GUDAO,
LONE ISLET
The War Years in Shanghai-
a childhood memoir

Margaret Blair

authorHOUSE®

AuthorHouse™ UK
1663 Liberty Drive
Bloomington, IN 47403 USA
www.authorhouse.co.uk
Phone: 0800.197.4150

1. Second World War (Pacific)
2. Old Shanghai
3. Internment (Japanese)
4. Chinese Holocaust
5. Nanking
6. Collaboration

Cover photograph © Fotosearch
Maps designed by Margaret Blair.
Graphics for maps and photographs of carved boy with
flute and the author, by Gary Moon

Published by AuthorHouse 04/26/2017

ISBN: 978-1-5246-7712-1 (sc)
ISBN: 978-1-5246-7713-8 (e)

Library of Congress Control Number: 2017901067

Print information available on the last page.

This book is printed on acid-free paper.

For My Family
Past, Present and Future

Also by Margaret Blair
Shanghai Scarlet

Shanghai Scarlet Reviews

Dually narrated by Shiying, the dapper, headstrong Chinese writer, and Peipei, a bright, sophisticated courtesan. Blair showcases the challenges the couple faces trying to build a life together in desperate circumstances …The novel skillfully explores the duty of the artist during wartime.

More potent even than the descriptions of Peipei and Shiying, is the rendering of Shanghai itself. The narrative exudes an ominousness that saturates the city. … Serious, informative and graphic, this book expertly plumbs despair."
KIRKUS (Indie) REVIEWS

"Richly crafted with nuance, this novel transports the reader inside the life and minds of the characters. You are invited to join a world hidden in mystery and intrigue, from war-torn Shanghai's dance halls and night clubs, to quiet backroom salons. … Complete with playlists – audio and visual suggestions – this novel is an experience worth the journey.".
US Review of Books

"The world of 1930s Shanghai is vividly brought to life in Margaret Blair's *Shanghai Scarlet*, which centres on a young man named Mu Shiying, a rising star in the city's literary scene. … In 1934 he meets a remarkable woman named Qiu Peipei. … Blair's book charts the course of their relationship as it winds its way through the wonderfully portrayed intellectual and social world of a city on the brink of major upheaval.
Historical Novel Society

"But it's the particular story of Shiying and Peipei that gives the novel (an amalgam of fact and fiction) its haunting conclusion. … A coup de theatre that could have come from the Hollywood movies that so beguiled the Shanghai audiences of the 1930s."
Lesley Duncan, *The Herald* UK

Contents

PART III: RELEASE

WARTIME CHINA
AND
JAPAN / THE PACIFIC

USSR

MANCHURIA

Peking

Wei Hai Wei

NORTH
KOREA

SOUTH
KOREA

Sea
of
Japan

Hiroshima

Yellow
Sea

Nanking

Nagasaki

Shanghai

Yangtze River

Formosa
(Taiwan)

Hong Kong

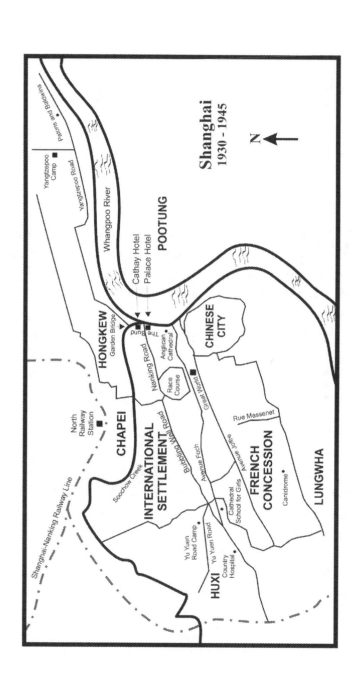

Shanghai
1930 – 1945

N

Patons and Baldwins
Yangtzepoo Camp
Yangtzepoo Road
Whangpoo River
Cathay Hotel
Palace Hotel
POOTUNG
HONGKEW
Garden Bridge
The Bund
Nanking Road
Anglican Cathedral
CHINESE CITY
Race Course
Great World
Rue Massenet
North Railway Station
CHAPEI
INTERNATIONAL SETTLEMENT
Soochow Creek
Bubbling Well Road
Avenue Foch
Avenue Joffre
Cathedral School for Girls
FRENCH CONCESSION
Canidrome
LUNGWHA
Shanghai-Nanking Railway Line
Yu Yuen Road Camp
Yu Yuen Road
Country Hospital
HUXI

Preface

From time to time, a city steps on to the world stage as the embodiment of modernity to which people flock for entertainment and fame, power, money and limitless opportunity. In the 1930s the International Settlement of Shanghai was such a place.

In Shanghai the Nationalists overthrew the Manchu dynasty in 1912 and established the Republic of China. Shanghai was also the birthplace of the Chinese Communist Party in 1921. Peking held sway as the centre of governmental authority, but the whole of China looked to Shanghai for the latest in business, fashion, literature, movies, entertainment and urban design. By the time of this story, much of the Treaty Port of Shanghai was built in the Art Deco style. It was a city ahead of its time, a mosaic of many different ethnic groups, a hotbed of spying and power plays, a fine place for rackets, drugs and international business, a crossroads of empire.

After their 1931 invasion of Manchuria, in raids reaching the Chinese area of Shanghai, the Japanese became the first power to bomb civilians during the 1930s. European nations passed trade embargoes against Japan in an unsuccessful attempt to stop the massacres and terrorization of Chinese civilians. By the summer of 1937, the Japanese imperial forces had reached Shanghai. Within a few days, millions of terrified Chinese civilians surged across the Garden Bridge, exploding throughout the foreign concessions and trebling the population to four million. Treaty Port authorities closed off all entries.

By insisting on adherence to the clause in the Land Regulations governing foreign concessions: that each ethnic group must look after its own, the Nationalist leader Chiang Kai-shek hampered relief efforts. In the Treaty Port, Chinese workers frantically built extra floors at mid-height across rooms in existing Chinese occupied houses, refugees slept in offices and warehouses. However, by the end of the year, in the International Settlement alone, the Chinese Benevolent Society had removed over 100,000 bodies from the streets.

The takeover of the Chinese area of the city affected the Settlement in another way when two bombs, inexpertly aimed by the Chinese air force, tore into the afternoon crowd on the main thoroughfare of Nanking Road, a continuation of Bubbling Well Road where we lived in a walled British compound. Over 2,000 people died, and hundreds of dismembered bodies lay outside the glamorous hotels and restaurants amid the shards of the wrecked neon signs.

After this tragic bombing, the British government withdrew its citizens from Shanghai to safety in Hong Kong, but returned them when fighting had died down. Meanwhile, in Nanking, Japanese forces murdered by hand over twice as many people as were later killed in the final tragedy of the war: the atomic bombings of Hiroshima and Nagasaki.

As storm clouds gathered over Britain and its colonies, and over the European allies and Japan, in particular after the declaration of war in Europe, British officials forming the backbone of government in the International Settlement of Shanghai resigned and prepared to leave. They would take their families to safer places in the Commonwealth, and offer their services there, on Allied territory, for the coming conflict.

But now the Settlement found itself tightly drawn into the embrace of the British Empire. British Ambassador Sir Archibald Clark Kerr (later Lord Inverchapel) began addressing groups of British Shanghai Municipal Council officials, and in particular the police, to persuade them that it was their duty to the Empire (not to mention the substantial British commercial stake in Shanghai) to stay and preserve order. In speaking with individuals he allowed the word treason to enter the conversation.

In 1941, when they attacked Pearl Harbor the Japanese started a war that left behind it unresolved and important issues having implications for the present day. At the same time the Japanese forcibly took over places of strategic importance such as the *gudao,* lone islet, of safety provided by the neutral International Settlement. The legendary vitality of Shanghai that the Chinese called *jenao* or hot din came to a stop. This story begins a few months before the December 1941 Japanese attack.

I write to inform, and also to bear witness about what happened during the Japanese invasion: the in-fighting between Nationalist and Communist Chinese and the inconceivably cruel ordeal of the Chinese civilians. My childhood memories, reinforced by discussions with others who were there and recent historical research, make this a work of non-fiction. I trust the story will strike a chord with fellow survivors.

The historical background is not meant to provide a comprehensive history but is there to add depth to the child's narrative. Also, I have used the Wade-Giles spelling for Chinese words and names, as these were current in the time span covered in the book. The change to Pinyin took place in 1958. For instance, Peking is now Beijing. In writing about my early life I have used British, rather than North American wording – as that is what we used then.

There are several, easily identifiable fictionalized accounts of actual events and also see pages 79 (old man drowning) and 108 (greeting to the Japanese Emperor).

Margaret Blair (née Telfer), Canada

NOTE the photograph below of the soapstone carving of a boy playing a flute. The front view is on the title page and the back view is on the page immediately after the end of the story. This was a present from my beloved Amah, Ah Ling, after the end of the war. It features in the same positions in my second book, *Shanghai Scarlet*. In that book it is also a gift, chosen by Qiu Peipei and given by her true love, Mu Shiying

PART I
PRELUDE

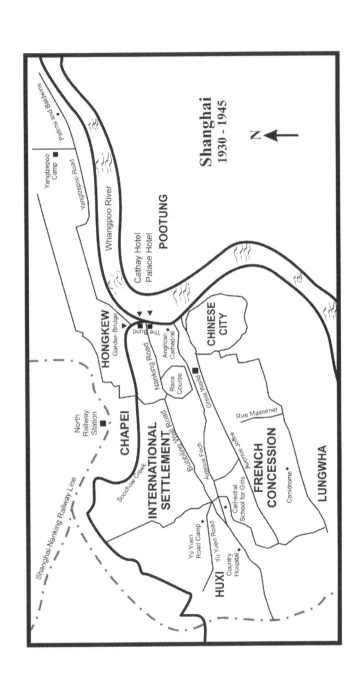

Shanghai 1930 - 1945

1. Our Family

I woke up from my afternoon nap to the gentle attentions of Amah: my nurse, the centre of my life, my Chinese mother. She opened the window, and came over to stroke my face while I stretched in the bed my father had ordered from a Chinese workshop. It was the colour of chocolate, with slatted arms coming down half way on either side. The first thing I saw when I opened my eyes, was Mickey Mouse, carved on the footboard and painted in bright colours. Donald Duck was carved on the headboard, and Pluto sat up on the reverse side at the foot of the bed.

Once I was awake, Amah gave me a drink of milk in bed; then she took me to the bathroom for a wash and change into day clothes. As we went downstairs, I was aware of the acrid aroma of joss sticks. I remembered my mother telling me that this meant that Amah and Ah Fok, who ran our house, must have been praying in their own way, just as we prayed in ours at Shanghai's Anglican Holy Trinity Cathedral where we went to church on Sundays. The living room to the right of the stairs was cold, as Ah Fok had opened the windows and French doors to the garden to dispel the scent. He was busy lighting the fire to warm the place before everyone else returned later in the afternoon.

1

Amah led me through the hall and downstairs to the kitchen. To allow for the floods from the Yangtze, which sometimes seeped in to this lowest level of the house in the spring, it had stone floors and no cupboards at floor level. But the room was warm. Ah Fok had just taken a batch of small cakes for tea from the oven, and they were cooling on a rack at the large wooden table where he prepared food, and where Ah Fok and Ah Ling, my amah, sat to have their meals.

The aroma of cakes mixed with the scent of the food the others had been eating. Amah still had some left in a bowl on the table. She took me on her knee and I leaned against her shoulder as she fed me delicious rice and vegetables, with chopsticks, from her bowl. I loved the crunch of the bamboo shoots and the spicy taste of the baby bok choi and rice with soya sauce.

In the dim light of our kitchen in Bubbling Well Road, some of Ah Fok's relatives were sitting round the table, finishing their meal. I was almost lulled back to sleep listening to their conversation, which I did not understand, but which flowed easily and quietly along, spoken in the comfortable, sibilant dialect of Shanghai. When I'd finished eating, Ah Fok's wife came round the table and popped a piece of warm cake into my mouth. She stroked my hair.

Just then we heard my mother arriving home from lunch and a game of *mah jong* with friends. She thanked the rickshaw coolie as she paid him for the ride. Then Ah Fok took her coat, crossed the hall's polished wooden floor, and hung the garment in the cupboard beside the stairs down to the kitchen. Ah Ling washed my face, and helped me up the stairs and through the hall into the living room, where my mother sat in one of the fat, comfortable armchairs in front of the fire. Ah Fok had closed the doors and windows and drawn the curtains in the dining room alcove off the living room. There was a lamp on beside my mother's chair, and the fire gave a cheerful glow. I ran to climb on her knee. One of our dogs, Dopey, an old English bulldog, was asleep in his basket beside the fire. He opened one eye and then lapsed back into his doze. He was called Dopey because he was part of a litter of eight, one of them white, named after Snow White and the seven dwarfs. Our other dog, a cairn terrier named Janey, was curled up in a corner of the couch.

"Did you enjoy your day?" said my mother as she kissed me. "What did you do?" I told her about the letters I'd learned to print that morning at the Cathedral Girls' School, where I went to Kindergarten as I was five years old, and how I had wakened from my nap. Just then my brother, Gordon, arrived home from the Cathedral Boys' School, and ran in. Giving Ah Fok some money to pay for the rickshaw ride, our mother hugged Gordon and asked if he'd had a good day at school. Amah took my brother up to wash and change out of his school uniform. Ah Fok was just wheeling in the tea trolley when Gordon came down again. While having tea, he sat in the armchair on the other side of the fire and told us about his art class, and the boxing lessons he was having at school from Billy Tingle.

"Mummy, we could draw anything we liked."

"And what did you choose?"

"A knight in full armour. Look, I've brought it home," and from behind his back Gordon brought out a wonderful drawing.

"You have your father's talent," said our mother.

"And I managed to hit Billy Tingle twice with my boxing gloves, too."

After tea, our mother decided to read a story from *The Golden Book of Wonder.* It was about the Golden Goose.

"There was once a man who had three sons, the youngest of whom was named Dummling," read our mother. This was too tame for Gordon, who decided to get some action by having Dopey do his one and only trick. My brother suddenly leapt up, put his arm out at a right angle to his body, and declared loudly, "Heil Hitler!" Dopey immediately woke up and barked and growled menacingly.

"Don't you think you can find something quieter to do?" said our mother mildly.

"I'll go upstairs and finish making a swing for Margaret's dolls with my Meccano." Peace returned.

After reading the story, my mother called Amah and asked her to put on my coat and send me down to the gate of our walled compound. It was time for me to go and meet my father when he returned from work as Superintendent of the Criminal Investigation Department (CID) for the Shanghai Municipal Council's police force (SMP). I waited until my father's black car, driven by a Chinese policeman, stopped at the gate to be challenged and allowed in. Then I had my special treat: I stepped into the back of the car and rode home with my father through the compound to our own house.

After he had thanked his driver and sent him back to the police station with the car, my father led me to the living room, picked me up, and waltzed round the room, singing a waltz tune, as if we were at a dance, stopping to kiss my mother on the way. When Gordon came running downstairs, my father put me back on my mother's knee, crouched down to Gordon's level and threw him a few punches, which my brother parried with his forearms in the approved boxing style. Our father laughed and ruffled Gordon's hair. He went to the drinks cabinet in the sideboard, and asked our mother if she'd like a sherry. I looked around; everyone was home again.

Sometimes our parents went out for dinner with friends, but that evening we had the meal as a family. Tonight was our weekly dinner of Chinese food, and we all used chopsticks to eat it.

"Makee fine food tonight," said my mother to Ah Fok, when he'd finished serving. Ah Fok and our amah, Ah Ling, lived with us. Their names were really Fok and Ling; the Ah in front of their names was a courteous way of addressing them.

My mother had made an initial foray into hiring servants who were (or said they were) Christians. Being a Christian herself, she wanted to encourage that religion. She later came to understand and respect the differences between us, as foreigners in the minority, and the Chinese. Christianity was not exactly the leading religion of China, and we had a series of incompetents coming, pretending to be Christians. One of these, a "boy" (male house manager) turned out to be running a protection racket among the compound's other servants, who had to pay him money regularly to avoid being beaten. My mother dismissed him; in fact he went to jail. Next came Ah Fok.

The Chinese Land Regulations laid out strict working conditions for Chinese workers in the foreign concessions of the Treaty Ports, of which Shanghai was one. By these

Ah Fok was entitled to two coolies, or lower level servants, to do the rough work for our house, which wasn't very large. But he was never able to get along with the coolies even when he hired them himself. So Ah Fok ruled our household, doing all the cleaning and cooking himself, and taking home his wage and that of two coolies as well.

The person with whom I spent most of my time was our amah (the Chinese word for mother) who told me her full name was Young Ah Ling. Amah came from the Canton region of China. She was younger than my parents, in her twenties, and had a beautiful, long slim build with a long, rather than round, face. Ah Ling was highly intelligent. She spoke several European languages, Japanese and Shanghainese as well as her own Cantonese. She did not read or write, so Ah Ling never read to me. During one of our talks, I promised that when I learned to do these things myself, I would show her how. But time was short and I never did manage to teach her.

As soon as my mother came back from the hospital after childbirth, and was getting out of the car, Amah seized me and took charge of my care. My mother didn't even bathe me as she had bathed my brother as a baby. My mother tried: she asked Ah Ling to set up my bath, but she always said it was already done. Ah Ling had decided to assert what she regarded as her proper place: ruling the children of the household. And my mother decided to defer to Shanghai custom. When I could speak, Amah treated me as an equal. I loved Ah Ling.

During the day, Amah took me to Nan Yang Gardens, to play with other children. There were swings and slides. Ah Ling was one of the few amahs who did not have bound feet. If some children were inclined to run away, they soon returned escorted by Ah Ling. She could run like the wind.

Once when we were sitting on my bed talking after Ah Ling had changed me for dinner, I asked her, "Why are your feet not like the other amahs'?"

"When I am small like you, mother put bandages tight round feet. When mother go shop-side, catchee food in market, I cry, I cry. It hurt. I take away bad bandages. Mother angry, very angry. She say must make feet small. I not like; I take off again. Then mother stop."

After we had dinner that evening I curled up in a comfortable armchair with Janey, a wonderful present from some friends of my parents who were returning to Britain. At six o'clock Gordon and I always listened to the Children's Hour hosted by "Aunt Peggy" on the local radio station, RUOK (Are you okay?). That evening the final song was, "Little Man, You've Had a Busy Day", sung in the falsetto voice adopted by male popular singers in the 1930s.

At seven, Amah came to take us up for our bath, just as the news was starting. It always began with a commercial for Jello. As we went through the living room door the American commentator, Carroll Alcott, started his news reading with the words, "Hello, Hello, Jello, Jello!" an introduction I always found hilarious. I went upstairs laughing and chanting: "HelloJello, HelloJello" over and over, just *feeling* the sound of the words. They seemed thicker than the jello, or jelly as we called it, that we had as dessert.

The Americans took their advertising very seriously. One afternoon Aunt Peggy, also an American, commented after an ice cream commercial, "Brrrr, but kids, who would

7

want to eat ice cream on a cold day like this?" She was promptly dismissed. The English-speaking children of Shanghai soon got her back, though, with a flood of letters and calls. My mother wrote a letter for me.

After our baths Gordon and I came down in our dressing gowns and slippers for a last goodnight from our parents. Our mother talked to Gordon about his day at his new school. Reaching nine years old, he had just gone from the Cathedral Girls' School to the Cathedral Boys' School. Gordon was learning French, and my mother heard him recite the vocabulary from his French lesson. Our father took me on his knee, and read from one of my favourite books, *Jeremy Fisher* by Beatrix Potter. I liked the pictures. I thought that Britain, the land where my parents were born, must have rivers and fields and flowers and houses just like the ones where the frog Jeremy Fisher lived.

The Cathedral Girls' School had many frogs that invaded the courtyard in autumn on their way to the school's pond. As my father read I wished the school had frogs like Jeremy Fisher, with clothes on. A troop of frogs in tweedy suits fishing in the pond would be an entertaining change.

Amah shepherded Gordon and me upstairs and I climbed in to my special bed. She tucked Gordon in and kissed him and then did the same for me. She placed my favourite toys: a classic yellow teddy bear and a royal blue stuffed giraffe, at the foot of the bed. Putting her hands round either side of my head (a wonderful feeling) she whispered, "Margaret go sleep well." I could hear the murmur of our parents' voices downstairs, the ticking of the nursery clock, and very soon I was indeed fast asleep.

2. And Shanghai

I was in China because my father, Alexander Telfer, after recovering from wounds suffered in the First World War, joined the Shanghai Municipal Council's police force. By the time I remember, he was involved in administration rather than in active police work. He headed the CID and later became an Assistant Commissioner.

At first my parents (Alexander and Florence) and brother, Gordon, lived in a house in the suburbs, on Tifeng Road, one of the "Outside Roads" beyond the boundaries of the International Settlement. It was conveniently close to the Country Hospital where my older brother and I were born in 1932 and 1936. Later we all moved to a tenth floor apartment in central Shanghai. But my first memories are of the modest, three-storey house in Bubbling Well Road where my family next lived. It had a living room and dining alcove on the first floor and two bedrooms with bathrooms attached on the second floor. A balcony joined the bedrooms on the outside. On the third floor were the other two rooms, one used for storage and the other as a playroom for my brother and me. At street level was the kitchen, which led to a concreted back yard with two small apartments, for Ah Ling and Ah Fok. Most of the time

Ah Fok stayed with his wife and children in another part of Shanghai and came to work for us during the day. Our house was near the centre of Shanghai in a British walled compound of similar houses.

During the early 1930s my parents enjoyed living in this extraordinary city. By then the British and Americans had joined to form the International Settlement which occupied over eight square miles to the north, in a bend of the Whangpoo River, with a common police force, judicial system and other public services: an infrastructure to support their trade and manufacturing. This left a smaller portion to the south, occupied by the French Concession, with the old Chinese city of Nantao in between, and the Hongkew, Wayside and Yangtzepoo districts across the Soochow Creek settled by other nationalities. All foreigners in the Treaty Port (created by treaty between the Chinese and other governments) had to obey the strict rules of conduct laid down in the Chinese Land Regulations. In return they benefited from "extrality" (extraterritoriality) by which, for all other purposes, they were subject only to the laws of their own country.

Contact with the rest of the world shaped Shanghai, which was a relatively new city, carrying little baggage of history or tradition to weigh down or mould its citizens. Citizens of the Treaty Port were themselves drawn from hither and yon in China, pioneers fleeing the civil wars and later running from the Japanese occupation, and the social and (often) economic constraints – even famine – in the vast hinterland, living and working in close proximity to the culture and customs of many different other nations in the international settlements.

The Shanghai of the 1930s most closely resembled present-day Hong Kong in its extreme modernity. *Modeng,* the term coined in Shanghai as a new Chinese word for the English "modern" or the French "moderne", described the splendid, complex and sophisticated city that epitomizes modernity in China to this day. In the early years of my parents' marriage, Shanghai had all the trappings of such a city anywhere in the world. There were broad streets and bridges, electric lights, modern plumbing, telephones, cars, streetcars, central heating and even some air-conditioning. Particularly in the four large department stores, consumers could buy elegant goods from all over the world at competitive prices, from Jaeger sweaters and Havana cigars to Houbigant perfumes and Florsheim shoes. An international range of leisure activities was available: *thés dansants, hai alai* (spelled that way in Shanghai only, elsewhere it was *jai alai*), greyhound racing, tennis, baseball, horse racing, plays, concerts and international movies (American movies in particular, as well as Chinese films, most of which were made in Shanghai).

In this place the Chinese named City of the Sea, young foreigners such as the senior students in the Cathedral Girls' School that I attended, had a wonderful time. On a typical weekend day a group from the Cathedral School (there was a separate school for boys) could go to a *thé dansant* in the Cathay Hotel's garden room, dancing to the resident band's latest tunes from America: "Just One of Those Things" and "Cheek to Cheek". Sitting in the 2,000-seat Grand Theatre they would have swooned over this music and the dancing from the Fred Astaire and Ginger Rogers movie *Top Hat*.

Then they could all spend the rest of the afternoon and

11

evening in the French Concession watching a hard-fought game of *hai alai* to the subdued applause of the spectators and the cries of bookmakers shouting the odds, and go on to dine at the Canidrome where greyhounds raced.

At the Canidrome grandstand, uniformed Chinese boys rushed along the terraced aisles collecting betting slips from gamblers representing all of Shanghai's many ethnic groups, especially the Chinese. The racetrack, with baskets of flowers hanging from the lights, was the centre of attention. Set off by the green central oval, the races were run in an atmosphere of high excitement.

After each contest, the elegant whippets in their bright racing colours passed by with their trainers dressed in matching silk jackets and white riding britches. Then the gamblers, many in colourful national attire – the Chinese in their bright silk clothes with frog closings, the Indian women in brilliantly coloured saris – took a break on the dance floor or at the bar until the next race. Outside, two neon advertising signs blinked on and off against the velvet evening sky.

The night could end in the downtown business district, deserted except for the Swiss yodellers bouncing their voices off the canyons of commerce. As the teenagers drove there they passed neon signs importuning: Please Drink White Horse Whisky ... Lucky Strike Cigarette Does Not Harm the Smoker's Throat ... Alexander's Shoe Store ... Johnson's Bar ... Visit the Grand, the Broadway, the Carlton Theatre, the Hamilton Hotel.

The Cathay Hotel's art deco spire dominated Nanking Road. As they went to sleep, the girls would think back to when they'd just reached seventeen, being presented to

British Ambassador Sir Archibald Clerk Kerr at the hotel. and then attending the formal dinner dance in its ballroom. This ballroom was one of the world's most beautiful, with rose-coloured curtains and gold-splashed carpet and walls, softly lit by Lalique glass fixtures. The girls dreamed of being whirled round the white maple wood floor in the last waltz by their partner, a boy from the Cathedral Boys' School, both of them cocooned in this fabled city of their birth.

Nanking Road (called *Damalu,* the Number One Street) was the address of many of Shanghai's major buildings other than the Cathay Hotel. Day and night it bustled with traffic and a mix of people of all races. The constant movement added a unique impression of teeming life to the streetscape. Chinese girls dressed in European clothes and high heeled shoes dashed about in the Big Four stores: Wing On, where my mother regularly went, Sincere, Sun Sun and The Sun. Not only Chinese, but also all the other nationalities shopped at The Big Four. The stores were so crowded you had to pay at a wicket for admission. Here, people could also dine, dance, have tea or coffee, view exhibitions of paintings or calligraphy, or see and hear a radio broadcast – and end the day at a rooftop bar or sleep over in the hotels attached to the stores. In Sincere's 114-room hotel, customers could stay in Chinese style for $1.00 to $2.50 a day, and in foreign style for $2.00 to $6.00.

The city overflowed with advertisements on billboards, in the print media and lit up on neon signs at night. The American magazine *Vanity Fair* became the favourite of many Chinese writers. It influenced the *modeng* Chinese magazines produced in Shanghai, such as *Liangyou* (The

Young Companion) that was full of advertising for a wide range of consumer products from food to gramophones and even to Dr Williams's Pink Pills for Pale People.

For China of the 1930s, the city of Shanghai, and in particular the urban environment of the concessions, provided not only a window to the West, but also the experience of living in a modern Western city. The Bund was lined with neo-classical edifices from the nineteenth century, but many travellers regarded Shanghai as having the largest collection of art deco structures of any city in the world at that time. This wonderfully energetic, light, optimistic, elegant yet playful style of architecture, combined with the American-inspired skyscrapers, built in the 1920s and 1930s, provided an ideal physical backdrop for the Chinese leap into modernity.

Surrounded as it was by the ultraconservative countryside, which was steeped in tradition, 1930s Shanghai became a magnet for writers and other intelligentsia from all over China. The city provided the milieu and stimulus for an outpouring of popular, philosophical and political writing, and for the development of a modern movie industry.

The ordinary Chinese did not live in the same way or in the same areas as those who were wealthier, or as the foreigners like my family.

One weekend my mother suggested I look first-hand at the other side of Shanghai. My parents strongly discouraged me from becoming a typical "Shanghai girl" who they regarded as generally useless, and lacking in any understanding of the Chinese people.

And so one Saturday morning Amah and I, accompanied

by my father's young Chinese policeman driver, went by rickshaw to visit Ah Fok's family. They all lived in a *lilong* house, which was attached to a long row of similar houses, in a compound of laneways entered by a carved stone gateway that Amah told me was called a *shikumen*. This *shikumen* had some Chinese characters carved above it that said *Xingren Li* (Alley of Prosperity and Benevolence.) As we entered, a Chinese man said something to our escort, and laughing cheerily went out to the road.

"What did he say?"

"He say he go get Number Eleven Bus."

"What's so funny?"

"Number Eleven Bus what we call walking."

Ah Fok's mother sat outside their house looking after his youngest daughter while running one of the games of chance the Chinese so enjoy, consisting of a dial and some upturned cups on a table. Several older people were standing around the table. A player paid the small fee and spun the dial. The nearest cup then gave up its prize: a useful item like sewing thread worth less than the fee. Everyone had fun or even won a prize. Those not playing were indulging in the most popular alleyway pastime: hanging around with the neighbours.

I was surprised to see a stout wooden bucket with a lid and scrubbing brush out drying in the sun by the front door. This was for the night soil. Carts came round early every morning to collect the contents of the buckets and send them by boat up the Whangpoo river to farms for fertilizer.

"Why don't they use a lavatory?"

"They no have." Amah showed me the seat with a hole in it, curtained off from the main house, where another bucket lay under the seat. She said the family was fortunate to have two night soil buckets to change round each day.

"For water do they have to use the well we saw when we came in?"

"We go see tap outside."

Amah explained that alleyway life reminded her of her village in Canton where they woke up every morning to the cries of roosters and the smell of the night soil wagon and small coal fires. Just as in the village, here hens scratched in the dirt, and coal burned in small tin containers to cook the breakfast of rice and pickled vegetables. In a few streets the alleys, so different from the streets I knew, gave their residents all they needed for their lives.

"Come see."

We walked around the compound and saw a street barber, his customer swathed in a pristine white sheet, and heard the cry of a nearby street food vendor dispensing noodle soup and fresh won ton dumplings to order. At the end of Ah Fok's alleyway sat a scribe in a long black gown, reading a letter and then penning a reply – for a fee. Nearby sat a basket mender working away. A seller of toilet paper zoomed by on his bike, and a knife grinder wandered along calling out for knives to sharpen.

Amah and I passed various corner shops, one selling every daily need: offering everything from tobacco and currency exchanges to bed bug killer, and another tiny shop for sesame cakes only. Groups of people were chatting in front of the shops. At the rice store I saw several men queuing and holding large paper vouchers. Amah said they were rickshaw pullers too sick to work receiving free rice from the PMAA (Pullers' Mutual Aid Association.) That was a revelation. I had always thought the coolies had no resources.

"No wonder they're sick. They work all the time in all weathers."

Then came the next surprise: rickshaw coolies worked in shifts with a fair amount of time in between, when they went to tea houses or watched the street entertainers and listened to street story tellers. There was always something interesting to do. The coolies were usually unmarried. Where there was a family, the whole family except the very young and old had to take whatever jobs they could, such as making straw shoes or scavenging for loose coal fallen from shipments. Being a puller was a job of choice, and better than starving or being killed in the wars and famine outside the city.

Amah and I returned to where Ah Fok's family lived. I had seen Ah Fok's wife and parents before, having a meal in our kitchen. In their house they gave me Chinese tea in a bowl. Ah Fok's family didn't occupy the whole house, but had more space than most with a living room and kitchen downstairs and two bedrooms upstairs for Ah Fok's parents and for his own family. The other rooms were rented out to two families not related to Ah Fok. They were all out at work but even so, the place seemed very crowded, just with some of the women, older people and small children.

On our visit to Ah Fok's house Amah showed me the pavilion room above the kitchen. It had been open to the sky for drying washing and doing *taiji* exercises, but last year Ah Fok had roofed it over and was currently renting it to a writer.

"He at Bubbling Well Road, D.D.'s Café, talkee other writers."

The whole of the *shili yangchang* (ten-mile-long foreign zone) was open to the Chinese people in the concessions. They daily slipped from their own world into that of the foreigners. Shanghai's poor writers lived in the garrets called pavilions above the entrance passageway of a Chinese residential compound, or often just above the kitchen. They made full use of the opportunities provided in the other Shanghai, away from the *nongtangs* (alley compounds).

Authors went to coffee houses in the French Concession and D.D.'s Café on Bubbling Well Road, where a Russian balalaika orchestra, in evening dress, played. Here coffee and snacks were available at a reduced rate, in the less busy off hours. The writers went to *thés dansants* and to the dance halls. These venues featured as background for the stories of Zhang Ruogu and the talented Mu Shiying who married a dance hostess. Mu Shiying and his friend Liu Na'ou were ahead of their time in trying to portray the frenetic urban life of Shanghai by writing in a vivid style, setting scenes that could easily have been adapted to the movies they so loved to attend. Although the authors wrote in their native language, it was not unusual for them to be able to speak others, notably English, Japanese and French.

A few fortunate Europeans were able to sit in on the salon, at 115 rue Massenet, of the writer Mr. Zeng, whose bookshop in the French Concession was a magnet for (mainly Chinese) Francophiles. They could contribute to discussions of French literature in the impeccable French they'd acquired, often at the Cathedral School since they were nine years old.

The branch offices of the bookstore Kelly & Walsh showed the scope of international culture open to the Chinese. These branches linked Shanghai, London, Paris, Hong Kong, Tientsin, Yokohama, Singapore, New Delhi and Bombay. They showed the significant role of European influence from countries such as Britain and France. They also showed the special influence of Japan, which had long ago adopted the Chinese characters as the basis for their writing system. Some Chinese leftist writers such as Lu Xun were educated in Japan where they read Marx in translation. Lu Xun even settled with his family in the Japanese section of Shanghai. Thus the Chinese modernism and cosmopolitanism of the 1930s embraced both East and West.

Plays, recitals, cabarets and later films from all over the world came to the Lyceum Theatre on rue Cardinal Mercier, and the best Peking operas and acting came to Shanghai, birthplace of the Chinese film industry. When *The Song of the Fisherman* opened in June 1934, during the worst heat wave for sixty years, audiences packed the movie theatres for eighty-four days, despite temperatures of 104 degrees Fahrenheit – and without the benefits of air conditioning.

Although the Treaty Port section of Shanghai was under foreign domination, the Chinese who lived there managed to preserve their own style of life and language and customs. They used the modern conveniences and security of these areas to build their own cosmopolitanism and modernity, their own new literature and even their own new political order.

It was partly the physical surroundings that stimulated the Chinese intelligentsia. They provided a place to gather, to talk, and a marvellously varied and sophisticated setting for stories. It was partly also the literary and media backgrounds, the bringing of Western thought and literature to the Chinese through many translations in the early twentieth century.

While walking through Shanghai's foreign concessions, the Chinese could buy new or used books from the West and take part in a world literary community. One Chinese writer even remembered finding a copy of Joyce's *Ulysses* and buying it for only 70 cents, a fraction of the usual $10.00 cost. During the 1930s these writers also had constant contact with the schools and international translations of Japan. Authors, publishers and translators considered the foreign concessions, with their special Treaty Port status, to be the cultural laboratory in which a whole new Chinese civilization could be fashioned.

In the minds of the Chinese intelligentsia modernity served the cause of nationalism. What developed was expressed in the language of China, not in that of Britain and the United States or France. This situation in the Treaty Port was quite different from that of the colonies in India and Africa where indigenous writers tended to use the colonial languages, English or French. In contrast Chinese writers rarely even mentioned foreigners in their works.

Perhaps because of this environment, in the brief century of its flowering (from the mid-1800s to mid-1900s) Shanghai became the crucible for new ideas and change affecting the whole of China. It was as though the city was a time machine into which the Chinese giant had been squeezed. Pulled along by Shanghai, China rushed headlong through several centuries in one from the days of the Emperors to Communist rule.

3. War Looms

One afternoon in 1941 I had had tea with my mother and was sitting on the carpet behind my favourite Chinese table, looking at the carved panels reaching to the floor beneath the table's octagonal top. I wondered where all the bas-relief figures were going: perhaps to the castle or the dragon boat carved on the table's top. Then my father came in from work. I had been too late waking up from my nap to go and meet him at the compound gate, and waited for the big hugs and attention he usually gave me, but instead my father hurried to my mother and held her for a long time. They started to talk and seemed to forget all about me.

The word "Australia" caught my attention. I had recently seen my friend Lesley McLaren depart for that land. When the war in Europe broke out in 1939, a number of British police officers, including my father, resigned to take their families to safety and go and serve Britain in its Commonwealth nations such as Canada and Australia. But the British Ambassador in Shanghai, Sir Archibald Clark Kerr, told them their duty was in Shanghai. The implied message was that since British families in Europe were facing Hitler across the Channel, then British families in Shanghai should face the Japanese across the Soochow Creek. There was a promise of evacuation for the wives and children. My father in particular was told that for someone of his rank to leave would be virtual treason. The Commissioner of Police, Major Bourne, was constantly reinforcing this message. And so my father cancelled our passages to Australia.

When I found out we weren't going with Lesley after all, I cried bitterly. As a farewell present I gave her one of two identical bracelets sent by my aunt in Scotland. There was a pattern of thistles and heather and tartan ribbons on a background of moss green. The material they were made of was celluloid, a forerunner of plastic. Lesley and I agreed to keep the bracelets until we should see each other again. *Maybe we really are going to Australia*, I thought, *and I can see Lesley.*

"Unlike 1937, the government has no plans to evacuate women and children," said my father, "I suppose they are too busy with the situation in Europe. Hitler seems poised to invade Britain."

I listened for more on Australia but my father removed a letter from the inner pocket of his jacket. It had arrived just that afternoon from Major Bourne, the Commissioner of Police and, as instructed on the envelope, he'd brought it home to put with his private papers. He told my mother he hadn't had time to do more than glance at it, and asked her to read the letter out loud to him.

My mother looked at the top of the first page.

"It's odd that there's no date on this," she said. Then she started to read.

"CONFIDENTIAL
For distribution CONFIDENTIALLY to
British Members of the Force only.

As a British member of the Force you may be worried as to your duty at the present crisis; not necessarily to the Council but to the British Empire in its hour of trial.

I can assure you that until this war is over our duty lies in Shanghai." ...

Major Bourne's name brought back memories of a birthday party the Bournes had given for one of their two sons: Robin and Tony. The party took place in the garden behind their house, which was several times the size of our own. It was mainly grass edged with a few trees and the same kinds of flowers, pansies and roses, as we had in our garden or, as I was to find out, that grew in Britain – with the exception of morning glories, which didn't grow there, but which climbed up the wall in this, and also our own, Shanghai garden. The city's usual marshy humidity had taken hold and I thought that soon we'd be going away for our summer holiday.

Servants had set up long tables, and began to bring out the sandwiches and jellies we'd have for the birthday tea. In the meantime a piano sat in the middle of the lawn, and we were to sing. My mother, who could manage anything without music, played songs we requested, such as "London Bridge is Falling Down" and an enthusiastic rendering of "This Old Man". There were about fifty children, all in their white summer clothes and attended by amahs. I, a timid child frightened by the crowd, hung on to my mother and wailed, "I want to stay with you." So I was also in the centre.

Later we would eat, and share the huge cake with candles to be blown out by Tony Bourne whose birthday it was.

The singing ended smoothly, but the next part was rather different. A camel and a donkey were to provide us with rides before tea, and they entered the garden ridden by the two Bourne boys and by my brother. Robin and Tony rode in first on the camel followed by my brother Gordon on the donkey. This was probably partly because my father was inferior in rank to Major Bourne, who called himself "Major" in memory of a previous military career in India.

The plan was for the camel, followed by the donkey, to go in procession across the garden to the other end where the rides were to take place. Their stately progress continued until they were about a third of the way across, when my brother dug his heels into the sides of the donkey and went galloping past the camel, to finish an easy first. Children, amahs and parents threw themselves from the path of the out-of-control donkey and the party organizers had to quickly arrange the next part of the entertainment.

I thought about how, at the birthday party, the camel caught my attention. *That magnificent stately camel!* I thought, *Never mind the donkey, this camel is what I want to ride. But how am I going to get up the courage?* I wailed to myself.

Several times Amah and I went to the camel. I looked up at the huge animal. It seemed about a house high, with long brown hair hanging down its sides. It smelled awful. My heart pounded.

What if I fall off? I worried.

The camel fidgeted, and snorted and grumbled. I stared at the brave Indian handler. He started to lead the camel away. Everyone else had had a ride. Finally, I steeled myself, and Amah asked for a ride for me. The Indian looked down at me with contempt. He said curtly, "No. No more rides."

My lack of courage had lost the day – but what a relief it was not to have to face riding the (to me) *huge* animal!

As I thought about Major Bourne saying my father should stay in Shanghai I felt glad, as I didn't want to leave our home – although I thought it maybe could be all right to leave, so long as we all stayed together, and my father was not left behind. I thought of how he hadn't even looked for me when he came in, or even noticed I was there.

In the past months my father had changed. He had a different, less relaxed set to his mouth and shoulders. I didn't understand the change, but then I didn't know of the ever-increasing strain my parents had endured for the past few years as war approached.

Given the huge influx of mainly Chinese refugees an enormous humanitarian problem developed in the city. Individual Chinese hesitated to help because they believed devils had an ill or starving person in their power, and could transfer to anyone who stopped to give aid. If the person died, the individual who had tried to help might be liable to pay compensation to the person's relatives. And so, affluent Chinese businessmen formed the Chinese Benevolent Society to help the very poor. One of their daily services was to collect and bury the bodies of those who had died during the night. Some bodies were left outside the alleyways, wrapped in bamboo mats. The Settlement police had to keep order, even if it meant threatening starving people, since they did not have any authority to help them.

My mother had activities for her spare time. She made quantities of knitted garments for the foundling home along Bubbling Well Road that received most of my Christmas toys when I was small, as I did not play with many of them. Chinese New Year with its gifts and street entertainments comes a convenient month later than our own holiday. For most it is a family occasion when people come from hither and yon to celebrate together and honour their ancestors, sweep and decorate their graves – but not for the foundlings who were mainly Chinese or Eurasian girls. Funded by wealthy Chinese and supervised by nuns, amahs looked after the orphans.

My mother also supported the BWA (British Women's Association). Among their activities was the making of food for Chinese women and children in danger of being forced into prostitution. Chinese volunteers took the food to certain street corners.

Outside the International Settlement the Japanese army, infuriated by the strong and desperate opposition of the Chinese Nationalist (Kuomintang) soldiers at Shanghai, raped and pillaged their way to the Kuomintang capital of Nanking. There, for months, under the orders of the Emperor's uncle, Prince Asaka, the Japanese savagely massacred and terrorized the Chinese, whom they regarded as an inferior race. This Rape of Nanking epitomized the experience of the Chinese people under Japanese occupation. The Kuomintang army withdrew in front of the Japanese and set up a new wartime capital in the mountains at Chungking.

By 1941 Japan's well-equipped, modern forces controlled not only its colony of Korea that it annexed in

1910, but also the main Chinese ports and railways over a wide swath of territory round the International Settlement. The German-controlled Vichy government had ordered the French Concession to cooperate with the Japanese. Given their expressions of support for Britain's enemies, Italy and Germany, it seemed only a matter of time before the Japanese would violate the International Settlement's neutrality and take it over by force.

Of course I knew little of this that afternoon sitting on the floor beside the carved table. I was aware only that for the last few months, things had seemed different: the adults tense and worried, activities disrupted and the Settlement streets even more frantic and chaotic than usual. My mother's voice, reading the letter from the Police Commissioner, broke in on my memories.

"Not only have we the strongest official support for this view but if you will give the matter careful thought the answer is obvious.

I need not lay stress on the risks and hardships endured by our Fighting Forces nor on the local conditions, dangers and difficulties all of you are called upon to face. The greater the danger and the more trying the conditions to be faced <u>where we are needed</u> the greater the obligation to stick it out until Britain is victorious."

My mother's voice continued.

"I feel many of you may be influenced by the newspapers' laudatory articles on those going home and feel you also would like to take part. You must remember that such praise is very ill deserved in the case of men leaving jobs which His Majesty's Government wishes them to retain.

There have been exceptions and a few of those leaving us, valued men I am most sorry to lose, have genuine urgent reasons necessitating resignation at this time. Every case is considered on its special merits where such exist.

I fully realize the urge to go home and help and I shall be pleased to see and discuss things with you if it will be helpful.

In any case I hope this note will give you that substantial assurance many of you may need that every good British subject in the Force is needed in the Force and that personal and family reasons, at normal times worthy of every consideration, should at this time of crisis be regarded as secondary.

To some of you this means some sacrifice, but I am confident, in realising the situation, you will without further hesitation continue to carry your full share of our local burden.

You are requested to keep this note locked with your personal papers and not to discuss it in public places such as canteens and so on.

(Sd.) K.M.Bourne
Commissioner of Police"

I looked at my father who seemed to be thinking about the present situation. During these last months of 1941 before the Japanese attacks on Pearl Harbor and Shanghai's International Settlement, what the Chinese called the *jenao,* or hot din, of the overcrowded city of Shanghai rose to a roar. At our house behind the compound wall the roar was muffled, but in my parents' whispered conversations, which stopped whenever I appeared, I could sense the change. My mother seemed anxious all the time.

Now the International Settlement had become an increasingly overcrowded, endangered and lone island (*gudao*) in a sea of war. Neutral, like wartime Casablanca and Lisbon, it was a hotbed of spies, undercover intelligence agents and provocateurs. In the underworld, Shanghai's gangsters fought those newly arrived from Korea and Taiwan for control of the city's rackets, but the Japanese were also very determined. They were harassing the Western concessions and undermining the police, in particular my father's CID division of the Shanghai Municipal Council's police force, by expanding the opium and gambling businesses. In fact drugs were part of Japan's strategy in the occupation of China. The Japanese were handing them out to children as young as ten years old. A population of addicts was not likely to fight back.

To the west of the International Settlement was an area under mixed control, termed locally by the Chinese as Huxi, or The Western District, though foreigners characterised it as The Badlands. Here Japanese military police and the collaborationist Chinese police forces, notorious for torturing prisoners, were headquartered at 76 Jessfield Road, a house of horror. These and various foreign enforcement agencies maintained an uneasy coexistence with vague jurisdictional lines. In the Badlands and also in the more defined jurisdictions of the city, such as the International Settlement, criminal and political elements of all stripes in China joined together in acts of violence against prominent and ordinary people alike, weaving a web of terror.

Many courageous writers, who had turned to political

journalism, the cream of the marvellous 1930s literary flowering based in Shanghai, suffered during the terror. Mu Shiying returned with his wife from Hong Kong to take up the torch from his friend and mentor Liu Na'ou, becoming a journalist in Shanghai: chief editor of the *Nationalist Daily* an organ of Wang Jingwei's collaborationist government based in Nanking. Some people believed Wang offered greater stability in the long run, and was more honest, than the Nationalist Chiang Kai-shek and his relatives.

Gangs, probably sympathizers of Chiang Kai-shek, assassinated Liu Na'ou in 1939 and Mu Shiying in 1940. Many young Chinese journalists died this way in Shanghai at that time. The assassins usually beheaded their victim. They often left his head propped up against, or hanging from, a lamp standard opposite the offices of the magazine or newspaper where he worked.

"The Commissioner's obviously staying," said my father.

My mother was not impressed. I knew she was annoyed over an incident involving Tony, Major Bourne's younger son, who was in a class with me. The teacher noticed he had an extremely infectious skin disease called impetigo, normally affecting the very poor, and sent him home.

Perhaps mistaking the rash for prickly heat, Tony's father promptly returned him to class, with the comment that his son could not possibly have such an ailment (as impetigo). Given his father's rank, and rank was everything in Shanghai, the teacher accepted Tony back. Then the whole class developed the skin lesions. To make matters worse, my mother had been looking after me, touched her cheek with four fingers (a mannerism of hers) and developed four impetigo spots herself.

Just then Ah Ling, my amah, came to find me to wash before dinner, ushering me out from behind the carved table.

"Has Margaret been here all the time?" asked my father, and my parents looked even more worried than before.

4. Puzzles

A few weeks later Gordon and I were having boiled eggs for breakfast. I ate mine carefully not to break the shell. Then I turned it over so that it looked like a whole egg again – just like I always did to play an April Fool's joke on our father. Each April 1 morning he cracked the hollow egg with his spoon – and started back in elaborate surprise at finding nothing inside. (He always found it very funny.)

"What are you doing *that* for?" said my brother, who was four years older than me.

"It's to make Daddy laugh and cheer him up. Yesterday he was sad."

"Don't be silly, we're coming up to Christmas not April."

Amah solved the problem by telling us that our father had already taken breakfast and gone to work early.

As usual this morning I got dressed in my Cathedral Girls' School winter uniform. It was a navy blue gymslip with the colourful school badge in front in the middle, a white blouse and a purple blazer with the large crest on the pocket. A navy blue overcoat, knee socks and shoes finished the uniform.

There was a greater than usual fuss about wrapping up

warmly because the weather was dull and cold. My friend from the compound, Betty Kyte, was coming with me. Betty was a beautiful only child who suffered severely from asthma. As we went out to the rickshaw we were hit by icy spears of sleety rain that quickly turned to snow. The rickshaw coolie tucked us tightly round with a warm woollen travelling rug and carefully fitted an oilskin front cover over the hood of the rickshaw.

Soon, Betty and I were rolling along in a little warm dark world, safe from the cold and wet outside. To see where we were going, we peered through the side chinks between the rickshaw's hood and front cover.

"Look at all the beggars shaking their tins."

"Why are their legs so swollen?"

"My mother told me its something called *beri beri*."

"Why are they like that?"

"Mummy said it's because they don't have enough to eat."

I noticed there was a small hole in the cover before us. Through it I saw the coolie dressed in light cotton rags, running between the shafts of the rickshaw, soaking wet. His feet were bare and the snow was pelting down. The rickshaw puller's legs were knotted with huge thick black varicose veins.

From what we could see and hear, this overcrowded city's all day traffic jam was at its height. Chinese girls in high heels dodging in and out among the trams, wheelbarrows piled high with sacks of rice, furniture or even bars of silver – all these were being honked at by cars trying to travel along what, in any other city, would be their exclusive thoroughfare.

In their insistent singsong, roadside stall-keepers were pressing people to buy tea and roasted chestnuts to keep out the bitterly cold weather. Rows of rickshaw coolies importuned passersby to buy a ride. A legless man with rags wrapped around his stumps pulled himself along. Sitting against the walls and watching the feet of the passing crowd, were beggars. Some were missing a limb or part of the face. They leaned against the buildings shaking coppers in the tins they carried in the hope of change from the public, a few cents to buy tea or food to ease the pain of their hunger.

I thought back to an outing with my mother: "Mummy, can I have some money to give to the beggars? Could we take some of these people home and look after them? Can't Daddy send a gunboat for food?" I asked. My mother suppressed a smile. The previous month my father had complained to her at the dinner table that yet another missionary had ignored warnings about bandits coming their way, been captured and was being sent down the Yangtze in pieces, first his fingers, in boxes accompanied by ransom notes. The British had to arrange for a gunboat to go up river to the rescue. Chinese farmers scraped a living outside the Settlement, and in the winter banded together to pillage the countryside for extra income.

"I'm afraid not. We foreigners have offered, but there are laws we have to obey while we stay in China, and they don't allow us to help the Chinese poor like that," said my mother. (I never understood my mother calling us foreigners: I was born in Shanghai and belonged there.)

"But *why* ?"

"The Chinese leader, Chiang Kai-shek won't allow anything else. He feels that if we give a lot of food we will have some power over the Chinese, and he wants the power for himself."

But we usually did give some money to a few beggars.

I knew what Chiang Kai-shek looked like. In the International Settlement large photos of him were inside the big hotels and department stores on Nanking Road. The much smaller French Concession to the south was different. The Vichy government had ordered them to support the puppet Chinese government set up by the Japanese. The French had always had their own police force and public utilities, separate from those of the International Settlement.

So Betty and I bowled along in our rickshaw, for the moment safe from the problems outside. The coolie ran south, past some British and American sailors from the HMS Peterel and USS Wake who, with the Shanghai Volunteer Corps, guarded the Bubbling Well Road boundary to try and prevent even more of the desperate Chinese from entering the Settlement. Finally we reached the Cathedral Girls' School, which was built in the style of a small European walled chateau. Through an archway Betty and I walked into the paved courtyard where about two hundred girls lined up to go into school.

Our entrance door was at one end of the building and led into cloakrooms. Classrooms for the younger pupils were on the ground floor, which was lined on one side with high French windows leading out onto the grounds on the side of the building facing away from the street. Also on the ground floor was the magnificent oak-panelled main hallway. A broad staircase, with a wide polished banister, swept up to a landing.

Betty and I put away our coats and took our places

among the other members of the kindergarten class. I was happy to be at school where the classes were small and the headmistress and teaching staff knew each student by name. It reinforced the serene environment that Amah and my parents created for me at home. I had quickly begun to enjoy life at the Cathedral School despite my unsettling first day in Kindergarten. On that day the teacher asked, "Who can count to a hundred?" Several hands went up but not mine, as I had not been taught anything ahead of going to school.

When I came back home I rushed to Amah."Amah, almost everyone except me can count to a hundred. Will you teach me?"

Amah started: "One, two three …. Twenty, thirty, forty, fortyone, fortytwo …."

"Oh, I see. Easy."

I returned to school the next day, all ready to count – but the teacher never asked us again about counting to a hundred. So as to avoid being caught not knowing something, I decided to work very hard at school.

Kindergarten was an informal place. We sat on cushions in a semi-circle round a freestanding blackboard. This was at the back of a large, bright room with four sets of French doors opening out to the school lawns, tennis courts and hockey field. Other somewhat older children (about six years old) sat in desks in front of the kindergarten, working at their own pace under the supervision of another teacher. They were in two groups called lower and upper transition. The transition children, and possibly some of the kindergarten ones, would come together the next year in what was the equivalent of the second primary class, all having learned to count, read and print. In the meantime I was moved to a table where I studied, still under the supervision of the kindergarten teacher.

I was soon doing transition work but was not allowed to sit at a desk. I was regarded as too bookish and too shy socially. Initially, rather than go to play with the other girls at playtime, I clung to the hand of my teacher Mrs. Roberts (a small dark pretty young woman, not unlike our headmistress Miss Penfold). There were so many other girls all running about and making a noise. The crowd frightened me. Miss Penfold asked to see my parents and her prescription for this reticence was that I should attend dancing classes at weekends, to meet other girls in a more relaxed setting.

After Mrs. Roberts and the other teachers took attendance the entire school had morning assembly and prayers upstairs in a large panelled hall overlooking the grounds. On these occasions Miss Penfold sat on a dais with most of her teaching staff. They all always wore full-length academic gowns. She led prayers, read out any news, and delivered a brief homily. We said the Lord's Prayer and sang a hymn accompanied by the piano.

During my attendance at the Cathedral School, (September 1941 to July 1942) I developed an obsessive desire to slide down the beautiful polished banister in the main hallway. Our stairs at home had a banister punctuated by large knobs at the turns, and was no use for sliding. Today I found myself alone on the stairway as I was on my way back to class after having taken the attendance to Miss Penfold. (When I went to her office I was always very much aware of being in the presence of a truly awe-inspiring personage.)

I decided I was "jolly well" going to slide down that banister right away. The students talked a kind of English private school dialect. If we couldn't be bothered to do something we said we "couldn't be fagged" to do it. If we were tired we also referred to being "fagged out." A person playing hide-and-seek who was caught said, "pax" (Latin for peace). We were always "jolly well" going to do something or "bally well" fed up. Any boys, friends of our brothers, we referred to by their last names.

So I left the attendance book on the lowest stair, and went back up to start the slide. Just then the school's major domo, Mr, Lo, entered the hall. He inclined his head politely in my direction.

"Missee go get book, go back to class,"

He waited until I picked up the book and went on my way back to the classroom. Our major domo was a stately elderly Chinese gentleman. He was always dressed in a beautiful long dark silk robe with the matching domed silk hat worn by older Chinese gentlemen at that time. He was in charge of the Chinese staff and spent hours each day walking around the school inspecting their work, and presumably stopping girls from sliding down the banister. I never did manage that slide, and for a long time I regretted it.

That afternoon we had a singing session, grouped around the piano in the Cathedral School's upper hall. We were learning to sing carols for the Christmas school assembly. This time we sang "Good King Wenceslas" – and the snow really did "lay round about" our castle school. As we sang I imagined King Wenceslas looking out from very much the same kind of window in the same kind of hall as we were in at that moment. I wondered whether the king came from my parents' land, Britain, which I had never visited. I didn't think it strange to imagine him plodding with his page through the snowy grounds of our castle school.

When outside our compound I moved in a straight line, travelling across the sea of "other" by rickshaw, by car or on foot with Amah. My world seen from the point of view of a child of five, seemed to be a series of islands of what I conceived to be Britishness, of which our compound was one and the Cathedral Girls' School was another.

The Cathedral Girls' School students went for field trips in Shanghai. One morning they could have strolled round Zikawei Cathedral. There was this deep sense of awe at the height and space and sheer holiness of it. On a later outing in Scotland, my father's birthplace, I had the same feeling of being in a holy place, but in a very different edifice: the little eleventh century chapel of Queen Margaret in Edinburgh castle. The Buddhist temple on Bubbling Well Road, near where I lived, produced the same effect. It seems that the thoughts of many people over time had left behind a trace, an atmosphere from their praying.

The walk took the students past Chinese seminarians solemnly discussing knotty religious problems in fluent Latin that the visiting girls understood thanks to their own studies at the Cathedral Girls' School. There were buildings entirely given over to language studies. The Jesuit manuals taught many Europeans the fundamentals of the Chinese language.

The visit to Zikawei included a tour to observe the Jesuits at their meteorological station. There was little in the way of charts and instruments, though there were a mercury thermometer and barometer with a large map of the China coast on the wall; but the observatory also resembled a giant broadcasting station with information about wind direction and speeds, temperatures and cloud formations coming in from the larger area in China, but also from throughout the world, by telegraph in Morse code, as well as through a rather crackly radio system. Here the Jesuit experts discussed the information and scanned the chart of the coastline. Simultaneously the priests were using all means to give the weather information back out to vessels thronging the China Sea.

A huge book lay proudly displayed under glass. It was the work of the Jesuit Louis Froc who had died in 1932. The work was an *Atlas of the Tracks of 620 Typhoons 1893-1919*.

The sleety rain continued during the day. At the end of school, Betty and I went to find our rickshaw to return home. Shanghai's rickshaw coolies knew all the foreigners by name, and our one would know us when he saw us again. On our return, as I ran in to see my mother and Amah I saw that my father was already there, which was unusual. I heard him say that the others had decided my father was to take a place as an acting assistant commissioner until Bourne returned from the leave he had suddenly decided to take. However, the rumour was that Bourne was not returning to his post. Then my parents saw me and changed the subject. I thought they looked very worried, but my father smiled and gave me a big hug. He went to the sideboard, where he had put the chocolate bars he always bought on Fridays. There seemed to be more chocolate bars and sweets than usual. I thought we'd also have more silver wrapping paper to save for the war effort.

Appearing worried was not typical of my wonderful father. He always seemed to be smiling and laughing and enjoying his life. He was also an intelligent, resourceful man. As a part of his job he knew how to speak Shanghainese, the Shanghai Chinese dialect, and read Mandarin. And while my father was a gentle patient person, his job also required that he be able to handle a gun and he had one in a bedroom drawer, which was kept locked.

That evening after dinner we all played a new card game about cars. It was called Touring. As Gordon and I went up to bed with Amah I turned and saw my parents bending anxiously over the radio listening to the news, only it wasn't Carroll Alcott broadcasting, it was someone new. Another person had left Shanghai.

5. Worries

The next morning Amah and I went walking down Bubbling Well Road, which was the western part of Nanking Road, Shanghai's main traffic artery. To the east along Nanking Road were large hotels, such as the Park at thirty storeys high, and huge department stores such as Wing On's and restaurants like Sun Ya's, the famous Cantonese establishment. Amah and I were going to a place on Bubbling Well Road, which she told me was special to her. She seemed urgent about this – as if she had to show it to me before it was too late. *Before it was too late for what?*

There actually was a bubbling well farther along, at the outer edge of the sidewalk. Surrounding the well was a low rectangular concrete wall, ornamented at each corner with small lion dogs carved in stone. We hung over the sides of the wall. Ah Ling held on to me very carefully. Peering down into the gloomy depths we could see viscous, black, malodorous water, its surface broken by the occasional slow-bursting bubble that gave a malevolent wink as it broke. This was the original well after which Bubbling Well Road was named. When we returned my brother told me the bubbling was caused by a slight tidal motion of the

Whangpoo River, the river responding to the sea outside and connected to it by the Yangtze.

The dark well on Bubbling Well Road projected a tragic and sinister atmosphere. I was warmly wrapped, but shivered in horror as I looked down. Gordon later told me he'd gone there himself with friends and said that many murders and suicides had happened there, people either jumping or being thrown into the well. There were so many deaths that the authorities had covered over the opening with a stout, chain-link lid, securely attached to the surrounding wall.

This was also a religious site. Opposite the well was a temple which Amah and I entered. Immediately the huge doors closed and a sense of timeless serenity enfolded us. The air was fragrant with the scent of joss sticks. On a dais at the far end of the dimly lit building sat a large carved Buddha with a huge red stone in the middle of his forehead. On either side sat rows of smaller Buddhas, leading to the central one. Steadily and softly the red stone glowed across the vast space.

"Amah, what do you call that red stone?"

"It name ruby."

The majestic presence of the statue drew us forward into the temple, into a sensation of fathomless wisdom, acceptance, and peace. "Temple called Jan'an in Chinese. That mean peace, quiet," said Amah: *perfect name*, I thought *but I'm going to call it the Temple of the Ruby Buddha.*

"This holy place for very long time, two thousand year," said Amah "Here many Chinese people think of Buddha; they pray," said Amah. As Ah Ling probably suspected, the events of the war were soon to overtake us, and we never returned to that memorable place.

After our visit to the temple we went straight home. I always found the walk along Bubbling Well Road exhilarating. The road had a personality of its own. It was much noisier than the quiet enclave of our compound. It also played out a heady life-and-death type of drama. The traffic roared along in a densely knotted, rank mass of different types of vehicle and pedestrians, trying to move at different speeds, rubbing and chafing at each other. There were rickshaw coolies and cyclists, shouting and jostling, pedicabs and cars, with drivers blaring horns to clear the way, and pedestrians weaving in and out, some with loads slung at either end of poles across their shoulders.

Occasionally, Chinese pedestrians added to the stress for drivers by "cheating the devil." This involved running out in front of a car and back again before it hit you. Returning safely from the roadway meant that you had built up your store of luck. Brakes squealed as the frantic drivers did their best to avoid running over the daredevils.

Tramcars clanged their bells urgently. The third class section (for Chinese) was filled to overflowing with people hanging on the outside, while at the front the first and second-class sections (for whites and wealthy Chinese respectively) were moderately empty. Shanghai was the first city in the world to install traffic lights; but neither these nor the Sikh policemen on the elevated traffic islands in the middle of the road seemed able to keep order. Somehow the traffic roared and rushed forward.

As we walked back I smelled a noisome odour from a dark alleyway, which spoke of a lack of cleaning and clearing of rubbish and old food. Then there was the aroma of the roadside brazier where Amah and I bought some roasted chestnuts, and the heavenly scent of peanut brittle made on a metal sheet — but a forbidden treat unless we bought it wrapped in a shop.

I began to think of other odours. I always knew when Ah Fok was around from his bitter smell. Gordon said it was because he ate a lot of garlic. A hug from Amah was accompanied by a wonderful sweet clean smell. In summer there was the scent of the anti-mosquito coils we burned when outdoors and the strong and (I suspect now) poisonous odour of Flit, sprayed indoors to prevent mosquitoes.

When we returned, Amah said, "Margaret must have rest, Daddy take Gordon and Margaret to The Chocolate Shoppe for tiffin and Margaret go to dancing lesson after come back home." "You very busy, must rest," she said again putting me to bed. As I fell asleep I wondered *why* there was this rush to do all these outings in one day. In the past months there was a different, frantic atmosphere about, and since yesterday it had become even worse. It made me feel worried, but I couldn't discuss it, even with Amah. I couldn't understand or describe it.

As usual, I did as I was told. Partly, I really did feel tired after our fairly long walk, but also our parents insisted we respect Ah Fok and Ah Ling. Ah Fok had been with my parents for a long time. He came once my mother had tried her hand at hiring "Christian" Chinese servants.

One afternoon I asked, "Mummy, why don't Gordon

and I know how to speak Chinese? Betty speaks Chinese to her amah. Couldn't Ah Ling and Ah Fok teach us?"

"I asked them to teach you, but they refused, saying they would rather speak English all the time. They *are* professionals at what they do; we need them for the smooth running of our lives, and so I have to accept this. Amah comes from Canton, but you would have spoken in the Shanghai dialect. China has many different ways of speaking Chinese, depending on where you are."

At lunchtime, that we called tiffin, our father took Gordon and me to The Chocolate Shoppe, an American restaurant where we could have snacks, ice cream sundaes and banana splits. It also had a soda fountain. As usual, Gordon ordered a club sandwich. When it came Gordon opened his mouth really, really wide. He liked to see how many of the miniature pieces he could bite into at once. I had a special club sandwich with no meat, as I didn't eat meat. When we'd finished the waiter brought a tray of chocolate desserts to choose from. Gordon chose a huge slice of cake, and I had a mixture of fruit contained in a chocolate cup. This time at The Chocolate Shoppe we were constantly interrupted by men, both Chinese and European. They came and talked in whispers to our father. Even here, where we usually had so much fun with him, the new atmosphere was taking over. I wished we could go back to before, when people were not so worried.

In between his consultations our father did his best to joke and see that we had a good time. Then he took us back home. Gordon, who was second head choirboy at Shanghai's Anglican Cathedral, had a choir practice to attend – and I went to my dancing class. By the time my brother and I returned, we were ready for dinner by ourselves (as our parents were going out) and an early bedtime after the Children's Hour on the radio.

The next day we attended morning service. We took a taxi to the Anglican Holy Trinity Cathedral where my brother was second head choirboy. We didn't have a car of our own as our mother had wrecked it driving into a tram and decided not to drive any more. As we went along we passed through what I would later learn was the red light district of Foochow Road. This morning the street was filled with colourfully dressed and made up Chinese women. Amah said they were called singsong girls, but I had no idea what that meant or what they were doing out in the street. We entered the cathedral past a graveyard packed with beggars, leaning up against the gravestones and looking almost dead themselves. I wondered whether, by lying across a particular plot, they were reserving a place to be buried.

"Daddy, can I have some money to give the beggars?" My father asked the driver to stop while we handed out coins from the slightly opened car window.

The Cathedral Boys' School provided choirboys to sing in the Cathedral, and I attended part of the service before going to Sunday School. As the head choirboy had a cold, Gordon sang the solos. His sublime, confident soprano soared effortlessly into the upper reaches of the vaulted roof. The choirboys' activities when not singing were anything but sublime. As we returned home Gordon said, "I won a dollar at cards during the sermon, and while we were waiting to sing, another dollar playing tiddley-winks. Our marbles almost fell over the side of the choir stalls."

"Really, Gordon, can't you boys behave yourselves – even in church?" said my mother.

"Alex, you really will have to speak to him. What about when he becomes head choirboy?"

After tiffin and a nap, I went with Gordon and our parents to a *thé dansant* held in the afternoon by some friends. Everyone, including the children, glided along light wood parquet flooring to the tunes of Gershwin and Kern.

Gordon and I racketed around a bit with the other children pretending to dance, or doing a new invention we enjoyed called "Hands, knees and boompsadaisy." It involved clapping your hands together, then clapping them on your knees and next touching shoulders with your partner regrouping to do a waltz. Gordon and his friends the Grant boys: Donald, Alan and David, had a tremendous time getting the most noise and confusion out of that "dance". Instead of touching shoulders, they cannoned into each other and then staggered about laughing. "You boys *behave,*" said Aunt Ivy, the Grants' mother. They were quiet for a while but then started again. "Now then, calm down," Uncle Bill Grant told them next.

We danced with one of our parents' friends and had fun "doing the Lambeth Walk." Later the parents had their cocktails and we children drank sarsaparilla and listened to a record of Deanna Durbin singing "God Bless America". Then it was back home to a light dinner and early bed before school the following day.

As I lay in my special bed, I felt pleasantly tired; I thought this was the best afternoon I'd had in a long time. The adults seemed more cheerful; there were no sad faces and whispered conversations. And yet there was something different from before, a rather frantic, strained quality in their laughter. It wasn't quite right – but then nothing was nowadays. Everyone seemed to be waiting for something to happen – *but what could it be?*

6. Before the Attack

(Long weekend Friday, December 5, to Sunday, December 7, 1941)

The first school week of December went along in the usual way, but on Friday we had a day off to allow the older pupils to be coached and also study for their Senior Cambridge Examinations. That morning I was sitting in the kitchen on Amah's knee, when my mother came in to see Ah Fok about the day's meals and ask after his wife, who the day before had had a baby. But Ah Fok's wife was helping in the kitchen, looking very pale.

"Why wife here house-side when baby just come?" she said to Ah Fok, speaking in the Pidgin English that was the shared dialect in Shanghai.

"Wife catchee baby girl, not boy. Wife work hard now, catchee boy next time," replied Ah Fok.

My mother said this would have to stop, but Ah Fok was adamant; he repeated that his wife must be punished for producing another girl. My mother, equally stubborn, asked Ah Fok to make some tea for his wife, and give her something solid to eat. She said she understood that he had his own views about childbirth, but that my mother also had hers. Mummy reminded Ah Fok that she herself had rested in hospital for two weeks after having Gordon and me, and that she was naturally worried about his wife not having any rest at all. Later, my mother called a rickshaw to take Ah Fok's wife to his parents' home, where she lived with the children.

After tiffin my mother took Gordon and me out to have tea with the Grahams, who lived in the French Concession. Uncle Harry Graham worked for the telephone company. (We always called our parents' friends Uncle or Aunt, though we weren't really related. As expatriates we didn't have our extended families nearby and so others in the British community took their place.) The two Graham children, June and Malcolm, were also off school; so we could play together.

But first my mother took us by rickshaw along Avenue Joffre, the main street of the French Concession. We went past dance halls where Russian and Chinese dance hostesses were going in to start their working day with a *thé dansant*. A Cossack in full military regalia strolled into the Renaissance Café. My mother tut-tutted at the Russians who she said worked as dance hostesses and shop assistants or hairdressers – jobs that under the Land Regulations were supposed to be for Chinese people.

"But everyone turns a blind eye. What can the Russians do?" said my mother. "They have no money after their long flight from the Communists in Russia."

We then drove along Rue Massenet past a bookstore, owned by Mr. Zeng.

"Mr. Zeng Pu, a Chinese author, is interested in speaking French and reading French books, and he and his son, Zeng

Xubai, have set up a publishing company and have meetings of others who have the same interest. The Chinese of the foreign concessions can read anything they want, from all over the world. They are doing a lot of translations from other languages into Chinese," said my mother. "In fact with all the new ideas, that's why there's a thriving modern film industry here and many excellent Chinese writers of books and stories set in Shanghai. The foreign concessions and the new ideas have dragged China into the twentieth century." I wondered which century it had been in before. This was too much for me to understand. Perhaps Gordon could explain sometime.

"Can I see those films. Can I read the books?" I asked

"No, dear, they're in Chinese and I don't think they've been translated into English."

The rickshaw then took us past Rue Wantz, where the Chinese Communist Party was started. I knew the Communists were fighting Chiang Kai-shek, and that my father didn't like them. *Maybe all these ideas from all over the world are not such a good thing – and why is everyone suddenly telling us so much, and showing us so much?* I wondered. I thought it had something to do with the new, frantic atmosphere. I worried about it all.

Finally, we went to have tea with Aunt Phyllis Graham. Gordon and I, and the Graham children, made a train with chairs one behind the other. Malcolm was the driver and Gordon was the conductor. June took me on her knee.

"You're the baby," she said, "and I'm the mother."

"Toot, too-tooot," said Malcolm and off we went.

"Gordon came round, "Tickets please." We gave him some of our money we'd taken from the Monopoly set.

After a while I looked up and saw our mothers bent towards each other, talking in the worried whispers, which had become so familiar these days. Then we said our goodbyes and our mother said that before going home she had to go to the Hong Kong and Shanghai Bank. So off we went by rickshaw to the Bund.

The rickshaw drive along the Bund triggered memories in my mother of her honeymoon trip to China via Europe and India.

"In India, bunds are mud dykes to hold back floodwaters, much lower than the Bund we're travelling along." *More information: what could be happening?* Along the Bund jostled the usual throng: middlemen, brothel keepers, compradors, boat people, opium runners, singsong girls, workers, shopkeepers, monks, bankers, officials, policemen, priests, gangsters, taipans, gamblers, beggars, patriots, pickpockets, rebels, street vendors, soldiers, conspirators, actors, sailors and opera singers. Chinese, British, American, French, Russian, Jewish, Parsee, Japanese and Sikh; these formed the cavalcade of Shanghai.

As I looked over the side of the rickshaw I could see a second city floating out on the river beyond the Bund. Here, thousands lived their whole lives on small boats, cooking their meals at charcoal braziers on the stern, selling meat and vegetables (bought wholesale at the Hongkew market) to each other, and doing their washing in the river, the children being looked after by the family grandmother. Large junks with the evil eye painted on their prows, to keep out devils, wove between the tiny sampans. In the middle of the broad river, behind the small boats, loomed the solid outlines of HMS Peterel and USS Wake. These and the Shanghai Volunteer Corps of three thousand men, from all over the concession, guarded the International Settlement. (The British had withdrawn their force, of about thirty thousand soldiers, for duty in the European war.) As we went up the broad steps of the bank, I noticed the big bronze lions on either side, their feet polished by the constant touching of the Chinese, who thought this brought luck.

We returned to Bubbling Well Road just in time to wash our hands before dinner. It was a rather quieter meal than usual. Our father, who was usually laughing and joking, seemed preoccupied.

That evening Amah stayed at the table with me. "Margaret eat," said Amah. "Yes, you must have a good dinner, dear," said my mother. *Everyone seems so anxious to see that I eat as much as possible. I wonder why? But I don't feel very hungry. I had a lot at tea with the Grahams.* I balked at all this food and didn't finish most of it.

And that was another thing about these days. Now I started the morning with a cup of warm milk, which Amah brought to me in bed before I got up, and then after that, everyone kept urging me to eat. It was a sign of the new times, which I didn't like and didn't understand. But I did know that *something* awful was happening. I could *feel* it.

That evening we settled into our usual routine of listening to the Children's Hour. Curled up in an armchair with my dog Janey, I heard the calm words of the songs and stories and ideas for things to do. By the time it came to my father's reading of a bedtime story, one from the *Arabian Nights*, I was in a more serene frame of mind.

I thought back to the morning. "Is Ah Fok's wife all

right?" I asked my father. "Why is he so angry about having a baby girl?"

"Yes, I've had a talk with him and everything is smoothed over. I've given Ah Fok a raise for each child he has. They are all girls."

"But *why* doesn't he like that?"

"Because things are different for the Chinese. The boys work and make money for their parents and take care of them. But the girls are expected to marry and take care of their husbands' parents. Ah Fok is worried he will be taking care of himself in his old age."

"Oh I don't think so. His girls will take care of him too."

We went up to bed ready to sleep well, before the active weekend we had ahead of us. It was December 5, and we were entering the busy holiday season. A trip to a film (*Snow White and the Seven Dwarfs*) and a fancy dress party loomed ahead for Gordon and me. I didn't enjoy these parties as much as I should, partly because I did not like having to face large numbers of people. Another reason was that I had to go to the party in my brother's outgrown costume. I detested the bright red pageboy suit with a pillbox hat.

A few days previously my father had sat in our living room before I went to bed.

"Daddy, I don't like my pageboy costume."

"What would you like?" he asked.

I hesitated; I hadn't thought beyond not going as a pageboy.

"I would like something fluffy."

"Like what?"

"Something fluffy, like being a snowflake or a fairy."

"We'll have to ask your mother."

But my mother prevailed and I had to go out that weekend in my brother's old costume.

At the party on Saturday, I looked at a huge pyramid of sandwiches, proffered on a large plate. I could only reach one of the lower tiers, and wondered what would happen as I gingerly extracted a sandwich. *Will the whole pile come down and drown me in sandwiches?* I worried. *Will I be covered in egg and salmon and meat and bread and …? Will they fall all over me and all over the floor, so that no one else can have any?* The structure wobbled perilously a moment …then settled slowly down towards the middle again. I was saved. After tea we moved to the living room, for a show of Laurel and Hardy and Charlie Chaplin films from Hollywood.

Sunday started as usual with morning service at the Cathedral. In Sunday School we had a story about the birth of Jesus at Christmas time, and started to colour a picture of the nativity scene. Then we came home for tiffin and a rest before going out to a movie. We saw most of these at home or at parties but occasionally went out to a theatre, accompanied by our Amah. This afternoon we were going to see a rerun of *Snow White and the Seven Dwarfs*, which had come out three years previously. It was showing at an enormous art deco movie theatre called the Cathay. We sat downstairs near the front, but I went under the seat when a witch and huge black vultures appeared on the screen.

"Why no sit?" said Amah.

"I'm afraid," I whispered.

"Come sit on knee."

That was better.

Shanghai was a major centre for Hollywood movies and shows of all kinds from the United States. In the 1930s and early 1940s, music from American musicals was available there, long before it appeared in Europe. So despite living thousands of miles away from the United States, Shanghai's English speaking children were thoroughly entranced by American popular culture.

The previous year, with Lesley and Peter McLaren, Gordon and I had been to see the movie *Pinocchio* and decided to learn to "give a little whistle" as directed by Jiminy Cricket. My brother Gordon, who already knew how to whistle, tutored us. Turning my back to him on the stairs I sang a whistle.

"No, that's not a whistle," he said sternly, "You have to practice until you can really do it."

Eventually we managed a first faint real whistle and even progressed to two kinds of whistling: through the teeth and through the lips.

Popeye also held sway over the foreign children of Shanghai. Spinach was the current wonder vegetable. To persuade us to eat it, our parents encouraged us to watch the Popeye movies in which the sailor man gobbled down can after can of spinach, making his muscles bulge and turning him into the strongest man around.

Then there was Betty Boop, a dark-haired teenager from a popular movie cartoon, with a cute 1930s American voice. The balloon-headed girl ran endlessly across a landscape when I turned the handle of a favourite toy I had. Actually, the handle turned the scenery behind Betty, who only appeared to be running. But of all the movies and cartoons I happily consumed in those years in Shanghai, it was the eerie Snow White that I would remember most vividly.

After seeing *Snow White and the Seven Dwarfs* we returned

home to an early dinner and preparations for school the next day. My dreams that night were confused and full of witches flying by on their broomsticks and sinister vultures waiting for carrion.

7. Respite

On Monday morning Amah brought me milk to drink in bed, as had now become the custom, and then I got up to have breakfast and prepare for school. But Amah dressed me in my weekend clothes, saying there'd be no school again that day.

"But *why*?" I asked.

"Margaret catchee breakfast and Mummy talkee," said Amah taking me downstairs with Gordon. We found Ah Fok and our mother sitting at the table talking. They weren't discussing the day's meals, but seemed to be exchanging news. Ah Fok had his sources from among the Chinese population. When Gordon and I came to the dining alcove Ah Fok went to bring in our breakfast.

"Have your breakfast and I'll let you know what's been happening," said our mother. While we ate she told us something important had occurred and our father had gone to work early. At dawn that morning, Japanese had attacked the British and American gunboats on the Whangpoo River, and were now in control of the Settlement. *So that's what everyone's been worrying about,* I thought. I began to ponder the situation. We always enjoyed our holidays among the gentle people of Katsusa in Japan. But everyone seemed afraid of the change in Shanghai, and of the Japanese soldiers.

My mother told us Daddy was organizing the police to help keep order. The Shanghai Municipal Council had ordered its personnel to continue as usual, and Japanese officers were now commissioner and assistant commissioners of the police force. My father was back to being a superintendent. He was out all day and didn't come home until after we had gone to bed.

The next morning we all had breakfast together. "There's a fair amount of confusion as the Chinese are now running away from the International Settlement because they're afraid of the Japanese. You should all stay at home until everyone becomes calmer," he said from the hall, shrugging on his coat.

Most people were staying at home. From the roof of the Cathay hotel, my father looked across the Settlement skyline. Beside him the Japanese flag, showing a bright red round shape in the middle of a pure white background, snapped in the breeze coming off the Whangpoo. Where before those of many nations had been, the red and white flags were everywhere. The red disk in the centre signified the sun, and the white background symbolized honesty and purity. Down below, soldiers prowled the streets. In a tight voice my father said to his companion, "Rape in war should be made a punishable crime."

Across the International Settlement a fine grey snow was falling: the ash from firms' and embassies' burning documents. For the banks it was too late: they were already occupied. Along Nanking Road flowed a long line of weary refugees fleeing the city.

My father was very busy but, as always, he did find time for us. Later that week he taught me to sing "I Belang Tae Glasgow" in a Scottish accent, and received a mild, "Really Alex," from my mother.

At first we stayed in our compound. But, with the help of the Settlement police, the Japanese maintained order and during the rest of the month there was an almost holiday air of relief. Now that what they feared had actually happened, everyone seemed to calm down. I was glad to know what all the whispered conversations had been about.

One afternoon, before our parents were giving a party, I went with my father to the Culty Dairy to fetch some Edam cheeses they had ordered. Our milk also came from the same place. I was sitting in the back of a car. My father was driving and I was dressed warmly with wool leggings on to match my grey coat. The leggings were buttoned down the side. My father had bundled me all round in a tartan woollen travelling rug so that I would not be in direct contact with the cold leather of the seat. (In those days there was no heating in cars.) The leather didn't smell as leathery as it did during the summer. Beside me on the seat lay two enormous Edam cheeses with their usual covering of red wax. The cheeses came up almost to my shoulder.

Despite everything that was happening around us, our lives seemed as comfortable and secure as they had been before I had begun to notice how worried all the adults were. I had a warm feeling of utter contentment.

Christmas week was a relaxed period; we enjoyed

spending more time with our parents, visiting friends and having people for a Christmas party. Ah Fok had put up an enormous tree, stretching to the ceiling with small gifts for everyone who was coming to our party the week before Christmas day. We even decorated a small evergreen tree growing in the corner of our garden. Our cake for Christmas was always the same: a large rich fruitcake from Kiesling and Bader, a German bakery near where we lived. It had almond icing covered in hard white frosting and a tiny sugar Santa Claus as a centre decoration. Because I was the younger child, my mother gave me the little sugar Santa Claus.

Christmas Eve was a wondrous affair.

"I'm going to stay awake all night to see Father Christmas," said Gordon, "So am I." But we didn't succeed. I woke up on Christmas morning to find a pillowcase filled with presents at the foot of the bed, and toys spilling over beside me on the quilt. My parents' many friends had given us all of the presents and some were quite inappropriate. At the age of three or four I was puzzled to receive a ping-pong, or table tennis, set. My mother's approach was to put everything in the large metal toy box painted brown, in the third floor play room, see what we actually played with, and give everything else to a local orphanage for Chinese children. The result was that we did not have as many books or toys as the other children we knew, but we played constantly with everything that was there.

This Christmas my brother woke me in the early hours of the morning when it was still dark.

""Shhh," he said, "Let's see what Father Christmas has brought us."

We left our beds and looked at the pillowcase full of presents, hanging by a cloth loop on the foot of each bed. Then I saw the most beautiful baby doll lying across my quilt. She was wearing a long winter dress in winter-white flannel, smocked in light blue thread, covered by a long light blue woollen coat with a bonnet to match. Both the bonnet and coat were trimmed in white fake fur. At chest level, there were three light blue buttons down the front of the coat, which flared out into a long skirt.

My mother came in, pulling on her dressing gown.

"You're too early. Go back to sleep," she said, and led us off to bed.

"Mummy, can I take the doll to bed with me?"

"Yes, dear, tuck her in carefully."

The baby doll joined my two other favourite toys: the yellow teddy bear and royal blue stuffed giraffe. The bear, a present at my birth, was kept on a shelf of my wardrobe until I was four and considered old enough to play with it. The blue giraffe came later, and now I had the doll.

During the lull after the takeover by the Japanese, my father had worries about the policing of the Settlement. In a heartbroken outburst to my mother he said the police were finding little Chinese girls mutilated for begging purposes. I wondered what "mutilated" meant but did not ask about this, as I was obviously not intended to hear or take part in the conversation.

"I'm going to create a small group to try to deal with this," he said. "The people are so poor they're desperate and will do anything to survive – even this. And there are so few police to spare."

In the past summer Amah, for the first time, had shown me where she lived in the yard at the side of our house. On the summer visit I had followed Amah up winding stone stairs to a bare room with a stone floor, which had no carpet. Her bed was low to the floor and had only sheets and a blanket with no quilt. Beside the bed, under the window, was a small chest of drawers on which were a brush and comb. I was very concerned about the bareness of the room. I clutched Amah's long cotton dress with both hands and said, "We must ask Mummy for a carpet and a quilt for you." She looked down at me kindly and took my hand to lead me back to the house – I didn't remember to ask my mother for the extra things.

Now she took me to her room again and I saw it had a carpet and warm bedclothes. Thinking back, I realized that in the summer Amah was proudly showing off her room to me. Just like us, in summer she took up her carpet and used thinner bedclothes; her room was nice and cool. Now she was showing me how warm and comfortable her room was in the middle of winter.

Unknown to us, Japan's official entry to the war had some broader effects. In Europe Hitler's resolve stiffened. He felt he now had an invincible ally and this strengthened him in the decision to go ahead with the "final solution" of the Jewish people and also others he believed to be inferior such as homosexuals, the mentally handicapped and Gypsies. Hitler's final solution did not reach the Jewish people in Chinese territory, notably Little Vienna in Shanghai, where the Japanese had ordered the Jewish people to settle. Perhaps their Japanese allies were too occupied with the complicated job of subduing Shanghai and the surrounding lands. The Chinese were their preferred victims.

From Chungking, Madame Chiang, who spoke fluent English, had been making trips to the United States to raise money and equipment for the Chinese war effort against what was now their common enemy, the Japanese. The Americans sent one of their most senior soldiers, General Stillwell, to Chungking. They also provided many tanks, guns and ammunition to the Nationalist army to begin fighting the Japanese, who had been up to now so much better equipped than the Chinese Nationalists.

After the fall of Burma in 1942, the Americans flew in these military supplies. The Nationalists and Communists continued their guerrilla warfare against the Japanese – but General Stillwell was puzzled to find that hardly any of the American arms shipments, to fight a full-scale war, were getting through to the Chinese Nationalist troops. (Chiang Kai-shek was reserving them for the struggle with the Communists after the war, and much American financial aid was being sent back to private bank accounts in the United States.)

The long Christmas holiday was all very well, but I was eager to return to the Cathedral School. The School was a major influence in the lives of my brother and me. I remembered how even before I attended as a pupil I was there at a sports event, running in a race for toddlers across a very short section of grass to a string at the other end, where my brother and parents encouraged me with their arms outstretched. As our little group reached the end of the run a teacher handed each of us a present. I opened the wrappings from a blue box. Inside was an extraordinary eggcup in the shape of a cheerful yellow duckling. On his back was a bright blue cup for the egg. On a later occasion my father distracted me from crying by using the eggcup to catch my tears, which he said would turn to pearls if we put them in the refrigerator.

At the Cathedral Boys' School Gordon had just entered a rugged environment where caning was not uncommon, in imitation of the English public school system. There were never any questions asked; if someone laughed out of turn or did anything else not ordered, out came the cane. The master took the boy up to the staff room to be caned in private, or, if the offence seemed serious, the headmaster conducted the caning in public, in front of all the boys. Gordon did not share my enthusiasm for school.

8. The Screw Turns

Our return to what I felt was a more normal atmosphere was short-lived. Immediately after Christmas, the Japanese ordered our family to report to a new headquarters they had set up on the Bund. They told us to be there at 8 a.m. on a Monday in the New Year "for processing." (For some this registration had started earlier in the month.) When we arrived we saw a few other families were there at the same time, so we had to form a queue. A Japanese soldier was enforcing a straight line with a bayonet drawn. I felt afraid; he looked so different from the Japanese I'd seen on holidays in Japan, so unfriendly. We stood for about an hour and my father carried me for part of the time.

When we reached the office, we had our photographs and fingerprints taken and were given a number. Mine was 0062. I hated the dirty black ink we had to put on our thumbs and fingers to make impressions on white paper. "Mummy my fingers are all dirty." My mother did her best to rub it off with her handkerchief, but the black colour stayed on until we were able to remove it at home. This took several washings.

After a long wait we received an identification card with our photo on it and were shown an armband with a large B and a number printed on it in black. The Japanese official said that later my parents would have to wear such an armband whenever they went out of our house, and that (also later) they would not be allowed to go to restaurants or cinemas in the evening any more. The armbands were a bright scarlet, *like blood*, I thought. "You must wear later," shouted a Japanese guard as we left. By autumn of 1942 all Allied nationals over thirteen would be wearing them.

I imagined my armband would feel rough, like the sacking containing potatoes Ah Fok made for dinner. The black number reminded me of the horrible ink for fingerprinting. My armband would take up my whole arm above the elbow. It would be too wide to fit round my arm. When we reached home after being issued with it, my mother would find a large safety pin to fasten my armband; but then I never needed to wear it.

I hated the armband's colour: it was exactly the same as the red of the pageboy suit I'd had to wear for the fancy dress party. Even *Snow White* with the scary witch was better than a fancy dress party. I far preferred attending films.

One Monday morning after the attack the Cathedral School girls were visiting the United China Movie Picture Company just inside the International Settlement near the Cathedral Girls' School. A Production Assistant showed the students round and addressed them on how films were made. Afterwards, the girls were in his office taking tea with the head manager Mr. Wong who looked worried. Didn't everyone seem worried these days?

"At (Chinese) New Year last year the Nationalist sympathizers burned a copy of *Hua Mulan Joins the Army*. It was so patriotic, such a success here in Shanghai and in the occupied territories, but in the unoccupied territories they say we are traitors."

"Easy enough when you're not facing Japanese soldiers. What are your plans for surviving 'till the end of the war?" said the teacher, Mrs. Roberts.

"So far we've avoided using Japanese film stock or capital, and even changed our name, but right now Mr. Zhang is making a deal with the Japanese film leader Mr. Kawakita. It'll keep our actors and technicians working, provide food for .our families. We are afraid of what will happen when the Allies win the war: will we be accused of collaborating with the Japanese? But oh, my dear Mrs. Roberts, what are we to do? What *else* can we do?" (Using his business and interpersonal skills, and also his wits, the brilliant entertainment entrepreneur Zhang Shankun kept the Chinese film industry flourishing during the Japanese occupation. With help from the moderate Japanese film-maker Kawakita Namagasa, Zhang used Japanese funding to entertain the Chinese during this devastating time. The Chinese had persisted in boycotting all films made entirely by the Japanese.)

After the holiday we returned to school, and soon Gordon had a real reason for not wanting to go. After a short absence from the classroom the Art master, Mr Radex, returned to find Gordon clowning around wrestling with another, smaller boy and accused Gordon of bullying. He then told my brother to bend over and caned him at length until he was black and blue. This beating could have had serious health repercussions as Gordon had recovered from a struggle with osteomyelitis (a bone disease) in his right leg, when he was five, but was not allowed to go in for contact sports, or to walk for very long.

The weekend after the caning we went to visit the Grants and played Bingo. For comfort, Gordon was sitting on a cushion. Playing Bingo was always more entertaining at the Grant house than anywhere else because they had a friendly Spaniel called Bingo. Whenever anyone called out "Bingo", he would come running and jump all over us. My mother told Aunt Ivy about Gordon's beating and made poor Gordon show us the black and blue marks.

Donald Grant told our parents that the supreme caner was the headmaster, the Reverend P.C.Matthews. He said Matthews worked himself up into terrible rages. The previous week Donald and the whole school had seen a fearful beating of two boys, Swayne and Sayle, during which the blood ran down the backs of their legs.

My mother told everyone that our doctor, Dr. Alan Burton, who was on the Cathedral School's Board of Governors, had put it to the Board that severe caning was not justified under any circumstances and that other forms of punishment could be more appropriate. They had agreed that from then on the practice of caning would be more strictly limited at the school. Gordon recovered from his injuries with no recurrence of the osteomyelitis, and we both continued with school as usual.

Ever since we had gone for our fingerprinting and armbands, the adults were even more worried than they had been before the attack. I wondered whether all this beating of the boys was part of the return to the times when everyone was so upset – and asked myself what was going to happen next. But I still didn't ask anyone else. I thought the grown-ups were the only people who would know – and they were so preoccupied they didn't have the time to tell me anything. My parents didn't notice me as much as they usually did. It was as if I wasn't even there. On other occasions my parents seemed over concerned about my welfare and health. People tried to distract themselves by "having a good time" while they were able, and preparing for the future as best they could.

During this time some of the seniors from the Cathedral School were sitting in D.D.'s Café on Bubbling Well Road. They had decided to go out as much as possible before rumoured restrictions set in. In one corner was a man in his 60s, well dressed and talking in a loud voice.

"Who's that?" asked one of the girls.

A boy answered, "He's Lawrence Kentwell. Was at Oxford and in the War with my father; a total outsider; stays at the YMCA near here; always trying to worm his way in socially at Oxford and in the Army; even tried to join the Shanghai Club. He's Eurasian. Can't he see he's not wanted?" His voice rose in indignation.

"He's been writing articles in *The Voice of New China*: pro-Hitler and anti-the British Empire. If one didn't disagree so much with the views expressed, they're really very readable."

"Isn't that Alan Raymond of the Independent Australian League with him? He's anti-British too."

"Traitors the pair of them."

One of the boys looked worried. "You'd better watch what you say in public – and keep your voices down." This dampened everyone's spirits as they realized the dangerous position they were in. The whole group went to one of their houses for dinner. As all cars had been confiscated and petrol for running them was unavailable, the youngsters walked. On their way they saw a long line of cars being towed along Bubbling Well Road towards the waterfront for crushing before being exported to help Japan's war effort.

Later, at the table, the Cathedral School group discussed Kentwell's life as they knew it. Their host said,

"The Foreign Office regard him as mentally unbalanced: given Kentwell's tirades about racism in the British Empire. I don't think he realizes how racist the Japanese are: that's the basis for their mass murders of the Chinese." Getting to the heart of the matter, the mother broke in, "No wonder poor Kentwell's paranoid: he's been persecuted so terribly, and for so long."

"When a collaborator of theirs is assassinated the Japanese have been murdering scores of ordinary Chinese at random; they are terrified. We also should be very cautious about how we behave."

One Sunday we were visiting the Grants again. Of the three boys Donald was the eldest, Alan, about Gordon's age, and David about my age. As usual their father, Uncle Bill, was smoking his pipe and looking very calm. Their mother, Aunt Ivy, was rather nervous and prone to tuberculosis. She was also a highly skilled needlewoman. It was Aunt Ivy who had given me the Christmas present of the baby doll with the sets of wonderful clothes. She always paid special attention to me, possibly because I was the only girl in the two families.

When we arrived Aunt Ivy said, "Run along to the playroom." As we went I saw her and my mother starting one of these whispered conversations that were so familiar.

First David and I had a ride on an enormous and very realistic brown rocking horse the Grants had in their playroom. Then we decided to play with a miniature farm set. It had dry-stone walls, as seen in England, and farm buildings and animals of all kinds. When David and I had set out the farm, Alan and Gordon started to bomb it with wooden building blocks let loose from toy aeroplanes.

"Vrrang, boom," cried Gordon dropping the blocks from his plane. "Here comes a B 17."

"Aak,aak,akk," shouted Alan, "Mitsubishi-Zero fighter!" zooming in on Gordon's "B 17". "A direct hit, you're finished," – and Gordon sent his plane down on the farm. "Kabooom!" *More buildings in pieces.* I went berserk, flailing my arms round and round at Alan and Gordon in what they called my windmill style of attack. Donald came to enforce peace, as he often did if Alan and Gordon got the better of David and me.

Alan and Gordon knew all about the Japanese and American warplanes. As we put away our farm, I remembered a fuss, which arose one afternoon the past summer, when Amah and I returned from an expedition with my mother. We found the middle of our garden, which we used as a croquet lawn, dug up into parallel lines of miniature trenches. My brother and some of his friends were using the trenches for a war they were fighting with their toy soldiers. There were soldiers pointing their guns from the trenches. There were soldiers firing cannon from recently created hills behind the foxholes and there were soldiers lying dead in the no man's land: an all too realistic depiction of the war outside the International Settlement. My mother had looked worried: more concerned than she would normally have been over what I regarded as just another of Gordon's pranks. Now I realized that she must have known the war was coming right to us, and have been afraid.

Gordon and Alan probably knew all along that the Japanese were going to attack. Why doesn't anyone tell me what's going to happen? Just then Aunt Ivy called us down for tea. Over the meal our parents were discussing the enormous crowds of refugees fleeing the city. They stretched for miles and the Grants could see the procession just one street from their house. I asked if David and I could go and see them after we'd washed our hands; and our mothers, in the midst of another whispered conversation, said we could.

Standing by the side of the road, we saw an unending column of weary, dusty and dishevelled Chinese, bearing their possessions on their backs or in carts. I had on a cardigan, which was red with white and blue trim: the British red, white and blue. The next thing that happened was that one of the refugees spat upon me, on my face and on my cardigan. I started to cry. David and I ran back to their house for me to be cleaned.

"*Why* did the Chinese man spit on me?" I asked my mother. I had never before met with hostility like this from the Chinese.

"Maybe they're angry with us for not being able to save them from the Japanese. That's why they're running away."

When we returned to our own house, our parents went

into another of their private discussions, their voices low and brows furrowed.

The next day the spring floods from the Yangtze began. The river overflowed the Bund and covered everything to a depth of about nine inches. We weren't allowed to paddle around in the water as it carried diseases. So Gordon and I sat on the broad ledge of the window of the landing between the main floor and our bedrooms. We leaned out holding strings, and bobbing on the end were boats Amah had made for us in paper of different bright colours. This window looked out onto our back yard, and on the ledge was usually a large bronze Chinese head mounted on a hollow wood base. My brother and I hid things there – until we found we were both using the same hiding place.

When the floods subsided, Gordon and I expected gardeners to come and lay down the lawn and flowerbeds for summer. Usually for a few days after the gardeners rolled out the turf we were not allowed to walk on it; so from the veranda we watched the cushiony grass. The humid Shanghai spring air sparkled with hidden drops of water, which reflected the fresh green colour like shards of glass. We dreamed of picnics and games of croquet. But this year was different. Our parents told us the times were too unsettled for us to put in our garden as usual. Privately they talked of yet another friend who had been taken north of the Soochow Creek to the *Kempeitai's* interrogation centre, Bridge House.

It was rumoured that in Bridge House at night captives, as they lay on a filthy concrete floor packed close to others who had been in confinement for months without being able to bathe, could hear the cries of prisoners being tortured. The stench from pus-filled wounds and excreta was unbearable, and fear washed over everyone. The windows were painted white and lights were on all the time making it difficult to sleep.

Captives who refused to give information, regularly died from the water torture so popular with the sadistic *Kempeitai*. Guards did not remove their bodies until morning. Prisoners had to squat on the floor all day except for four, fifteen minute breaks when all the prisoners had to shuffle round their cell.

On July 31, my father returned from work during the day, escorted by two armed Japanese soldiers. He told us he'd been dismissed, and his position had been given to a Japanese officer. He also said some people called the Trodds were going to be living with us, as they had been asked to leave their flat in the police station.

Hurray, I thought, and said we'd all enjoy having my father at home. We could play more games and read more stories than before. But our father told us this was nothing to celebrate as he was under house arrest and would have to stay in all the time. Unlike our father, our mother, Gordon and I were free to go out.

Soon after, our father read out a letter the Japanese had sent him. It said we were to clear everything out of our house and go to live near the Yangtzepoo industrial district across the Soochow Creek at a village that had previously been occupied by Seventh Day Adventists. They had built the village for themselves, but were no longer there. We never found out where they had gone.

Our parents had a special meeting with Ah Fok and Ah

Ling. My father told them it would be dangerous to come with us, but they refused to leave; they helped pack for the removal van that came. My parents said we'd be too far away for me to travel to the Cathedral Girls' School, as we didn't have a car, but that Gordon was big enough to cycle across the Soochow Creek to the boys' school, which was nearer.

I felt sad to be leaving my school, where I was so happy, but I returned for one last day. No one else from my class was going away. At four o'clock we said goodbye and I cried as I hugged my teacher Mrs. Roberts. She took me for a last walk round the school and up the panelled staircase to take my leave of Miss Penfold, that august person, who also gave a hug and said she'd miss me. Mrs. Roberts and I walked out of the French windows and round the hockey field, tennis courts and gardens; the grass had become green again.

Gardening in one's spare time was very much promoted at the Cathedral Girls' School. Every girl received her own little plot about one square yard in size and the teachers encouraged us to garden during playtime. I remembered sadly that the previous September I'd filled my portion with flowers, which our family's gardeners provided. And then we went for a last look at my favourite place, a small sunken garden at the side of the school. Gardeners had put in the perfect lawn and flowerbeds.

As I stood with Mrs. Roberts I thought of one afternoon the previous autumn when I was lying with some other girls under a tree beside this smaller garden. We still wore our summer uniform: a lavender coloured dress with short, puffy sleeves edged with white, and CSG embroidered in white on the pocket. Our panama hats with the school crest were tilted partly over our eyes. We were looking at clouds in a high blue sky, trying to put a name to the shapes and say what they most closely resembled. I thought that I would never forget that totally happy moment.

Before we packed our belongings to go to the Seventh Day Adventist village at Ningkuo Road on the outskirts of Shanghai I decided to write, or rather print, an account of my life so far. I wasn't afraid because my whole family, including Ah Fok and Ah Ling, and our dog Janey, was going with me, but I had a sad feeling that we would probably never return to our house in Bubbling Well Road. I had been so happy there. It was the only home I could remember and I wanted to leave behind something of myself. I could have left a book or other possession, but that would not have told anyone finding it who I was.

I asked Amah for help. She provided some lined paper and sharpened pencils. *What can I say about myself so far?* I wondered. I decided to print who was in our family, and included my parents, brother, Amah, Ah Fok and Janey our dog. I said where we lived and described our holidays. In particular I wrote about friends, Sunday school and the Cathedral Girls' School.

Amah waited patiently as usual. She put the final pages in a glass bottle and screwed on the lid very tightly. Ah Ling found a spade and helped me dig a hole in the garden. Digging a deep hole was not practical, as water was never far from the surface in our city. Every day those of us who lived in the city could feel the symbiotic relationship of Shanghai with the Whangpoo, the Yangtze and the sea beyond. As the day progressed, the edges of steps and pavements became slightly higher or lower, the whole place responding to the tidal flow of the China Sea outside. This great city with its skyscrapers and bustling international commercial life, breathed to the rhythm of the watery mud flats on which it was built.

Bearing in mind the nature of the ground, Amah and I dug about a foot down, and buried the bottle. I imagined someone finding it a long time in the future, and reading my story. I wondered what this person would look like, what clothes he would wear. Would the finder of my message be able to read and understand my printing? Would his life be very different from the life I had just described? I believed that I had written about a life, which someone someday in the future would read and find interesting.

The next day a removal van came and Ah Fok went in the front with the driver. I ran upstairs to see my bedroom and the third floor play room and then downstairs to the kitchen where I had sat so often listening to, but not understanding, the comfortable conversations of Amah and Ah Fok and his relatives. But nothing looked the same any more. The house was empty and sad. It was as if we had never lived there. I felt comforted by the thought that I'd left a record of our stay, buried in the garden beside the little pine tree.

My father called a taxi and we piled in with Amah and our dear dog Janey. I had one last look at the streets between the houses where I had run with my skipping rope and red scooter. We waved goodbye to neighbours who'd come out to see us go, and stopped the taxi at the gatehouse of the compound to give a last tip to the gatekeeper. He came out and said to my father how sorry he was that we were leaving.

We were all very quiet on our journey down Nanking Road to the Bund. In this early evening a bright, red and green neon sign on one of the hotels still proclaimed in English: LIGHT HEAT POWER, a symbol of the never ending commercialism of the Shanghai people. We drove past the usual polyglot throngs on the Bund, but the *jenao,* hot din, had fallen to a whisper. The crowds seemed quieter and more subdued than before. Now, the Japanese military whirlwind had swept into the International Settlement. The people were cowed. In his headquarters, Lieutenant-Colonel Ryukichi Tanaka, Director of the Japanese Secret Police in Shanghai said, "We can do anything to such creatures."

At the Japanese checkpoint on the Garden Bridge across Soochow Creek, a soldier pushed his bayonet through the open passenger window, narrowly missing the driver and my mother. We had to show our armbands and give the soldiers our identity cards. Another guard was beating an old Chinese man and threw him in the river where he struggled unsuccessfully to stay above water. A group of Japanese guards watched, laughing as the old man drowned. I looked at my father who seemed furious and at the same time worried.

"Why doesn't he just start swimming?" I asked.

"Maybe he doesn't know how to," said my mother.

"What is it like to drown? Is it painful?"

"Maybe someone will help him out," she said, but didn't sound as if she really believed it.

Our car soon left the scene and went through the Parsee Indian quarter on Broadway, where gorgeous, colourful silks were on display in shop windows and stalls. Then on past the Hongkew market, closed now but bustling in the early morning with stalls selling fruit, vegetables, meat, flowers and every kind of kitchen utensil. Like the people on the

Bund, the shopkeepers in this area may have been more subdued during the day because of the Japanese occupation, but everything seemed to have continued as it usually did.

I felt that in contrast we ourselves were totally different now: our lives had been turned upside down. We no longer did what we used to do; we were like grey ghosts passing through this real world of bright colours and continuing commerce. Eventually we passed the Yangtzepoo munitions factories and reached the outskirts of Shanghai and the Seventh Day Adventist village where we were to stay.

9. Family and Freedom

I sit on a wooden kitchen chair swinging my legs, and watch my talented father put the finishing touches to a meat pie. He has built up, petal by petal, a rose made from pastry. Now he smiles as he adds the last perfect leaf, marking the veins. The pie's surface is already edged with pastry rose leaves.

This kitchen has more light than the one in Bubbling Well Road; it has a wood floor and cupboards, not a stone floor. We live in a house separated into two flats. The upper one is ours and we enter it by a side entrance up a steep flight of stairs.

Ah Fok puts the pie in the oven and my father turns to me. "Time to do our multiplication tables," he says, swinging me off the chair, through the living room and all the way to the wide, shady covered veranda. Here we sit for a while every morning going through the material I would have been learning at the Cathedral Girls' School. "Seven times eight?" says my father. That's easy. "Nine times nine?" We continue with the game, remembering parts from the different multiplication tables. These serene times with my wonderful father doing arithmetic and reading together were to remain with me for the rest of my life.

The chill feeling of dread that skulked at the edges of our consciousness, with its staccato accompaniment of shouting from the Japanese soldiers, the stark glitter of their bayonets in the sun, the reality of our situation, did not spoil the experience. It could never dilute the essence of the few months my family spent close together with our friends and servants, Ah Fok and our beloved Ah Ling, free from the restrictions of the walled British compound, school, social occasions, my mother's committees and my father's work. What came after could never blight this last, perfect summer.

For the first time, I could step outside and wander unattended by Amah. At Bubbling Well Road I had had some freedom to visit other compound children by myself but there were always the wall of the compound and the watchman at the gate. Our new village had no such boundaries. Outside the last house on our road the countryside stretched endlessly. We could watch the rural families. Clad in black trousers, white tops and conical woven hats to keep out the sun, they did most of their work in the early morning or as the sun was sinking, to avoid the mid-day heat.

Not only did my brother and I have more freedom to roam as virtual prisoners under Japanese surveillance than as part of the British bureaucracy in central Shanghai, but we also had the opportunity to mix with the local Chinese. The village was surrounded by farmland punctuated by other small villages in one of which was the market for the area. Sometimes we went with Ah Fok and Ah Ling to buy food.

Here we experienced the reality of Chinese life outside

the European and American enclaves. We saw the teeming busyness, and life and energy, of a Chinese market. My brother and I absorbed the medieval extravaganza of merchants accosting us, in their persistent chant, to buy their wares: tin plates, fabric shoes and clothes, fruit, vegetables and live ducks, geese and hens, decapitated chickens that ran around the meat stalls sprinkling blood, (I cringed), the din and the dust.

We watched the itinerant players, musicians, contortionists, acrobats and jugglers, the seller of clockwork toys and mysterious gifts wrapped in leaves, and the dentist, his patients sitting in a makeshift surgery: a chair under a huge umbrella decorated with strings of teeth. The dentist extracted teeth with a large pair of pliers and no painkillers. One rinse from a tub of brackish water, a spit on to the ground, and the pale and traumatized patient went home with solicitous relatives. The next patient sat down immediately, head back, ready. I never saw any fillings, just extractions.

Ah Fok and Ah Ling were circumspect shoppers. They selected the freshest vegetables and tested the watermelons to see if they had been pumped with water to increase their weight – for there lay typhoid. We returned by rickshaw, weighed down with enough food for several days.

There was only one previous occasion when I had mixed with the Chinese *en masse*. Spring and summer brought travelling fairs to Shanghai, and one of these came to a vacant piece of land outside our compound. The front gate of the compound wall facing Bubbling Well Road had a gatekeeper. However, the side gate had no one to check who went in or out.

On a warm day, my brother slipped out with me by the side gate and we went to a Chinese fair. Going around by ourselves was strictly forbidden as kidnapping of both Chinese and Europeans for ransom was common in the Shanghai of that era. For a short while, we mingled with the Chinese crowd packed into the fair ground. We ate peanut brittle bought at a stall (another forbidden treat because of the likelihood of illness from unhygienic preparation) and wandered around the sideshows. There were acrobats, jugglers and small bands, performing and playing music, for the small change people would give.

And there were the stalls. However much I stretched I couldn't see the items laid out for sale. However, wandering among crowds of Chinese was a novel excitement. The people were dressed differently from us, in drab blue or black trousers, with tops fastened together by the typical, knotted (frog) cloth buttons. My main impression was of an endless series of legs through which we walked. Most of the Chinese brushed past us, busily going about their enjoyment. But when I glanced way up to their faces, I saw that quite a few seemed amazed to see us, unaccompanied, in the middle of their fair. No one tried to talk to us.

There was one show, in a tent, that we couldn't resist. My brother bought two tickets to see the Spider Lady. The body of the "spider" consisted of the heavily made-up face of a beautiful young Chinese girl. The spider's cloth legs writhed out from this centre.

"They're large snakes under cloth," said my brother, and then, "No, more likely broad rubber hoses being twitched around." The whole effect was bizarre and rather frightening.

Although separate, the Seventh Day Adventist village was connected to Shanghai by a road, which continued into Shanghai's centre where we had lived before. This was the road along which Gordon later cycled to school when it recommenced in September. Japanese soldiers occupied the large central building on one side of the single, broad main street. Ranged in a double row on either side, the houses were shabby comfortable duplexes (one flat above and one below) set in informal walled gardens. Ours was at the end of the village nearest to Shanghai.

In the plain front garden of our dwelling Ah Fok cut the grass and trimmed the bushes, an unusual task for him as previously we had had gardeners to do this type of work. The ground to the side and back was left to grow. Bushes and long grass flourished, providing a different playground from the more formal garden in Bubbling Well Road. Here there were no pansies, hollyhocks or morning glories, and no roses. I remembered the times in Bubbling Well Road when I went to the garden in the morning to cut a rose for my father to wear. However, here we had a fig tree. Mainly green but pink at one end, fresh figs are juicy and delicious – quite unlike the dried variety available in grocery stores.

Other British families like our own, some of whom we already knew, lived along the street. But we alone still had servants. They lived in their own quarters at the foot of the garden behind the house and came to spend the days with us, as usual, doing the housework, cooking and baking.

Our parents seemed to have a more relaxed life than

before, not having to go to work or parties or do voluntary work. In cooking, and baking too, Ah Fok faced keen competition from my father who, suddenly with time to spare, became an enthusiastic and excellent chef. He made splendid pies. I lost a tooth after biting into one of my father's rock cakes, causing him some amusement: those cakes really were hard as rocks.

After he had baked the meat pie my father set up his drawing board in the kitchen, which had the best light. He was sketching the scene from the kitchen window. My father had finished school in Glasgow, Scotland, at fifteen and was asked to wait for entrance to Glasgow University on account of his youth. Instead he attended Glasgow School of Art, as in his final year of school he had won a scholarship in a painting competition for the West of Scotland. My father studied there for two years and then went overseas to the First World War before being wounded and recovering after years of operations to repair shrapnel wounds on his ankle. His name is on the First World War Honour Roll in Glasgow School of Art. For all the time I knew my father, he always kept up his drawing and painting as a leisure pastime.

While living in the village I was able to indulge my hobby of knitting. Over a year before, when I did not yet go to school, my mother had responded to my cries about needing more to do by teaching me to knit. Now she brought with her a large supply of wool from Wing On's, and during this summer, clothes for my teddy bear and dolls, in patterns and stitches I designed myself, flew off my needles in all colours.

Gordon's hobby was making things. He has always

been able to run machines well, take them apart and mend them. Sometimes he would take something to pieces like our nursery clock or a music box, just to see how it worked, before reconstructing it.

One Christmas Gordon received a set of Meccano. Metal tubes of all shapes fitted together and several different sizes of engines came with the package. He immediately applied his skills to building machines that worked, and spent long hours with his Meccano set.

At first my dolls benefitted from an automatic swing with rockers on it. However one day after we went to live in the village my brother made a Meccano gallows and guillotine with which to hang and behead my teddy bear and dolls: I arrived in time to catch the teddy bear swinging from the gibbet.

"Amah", I wailed, "Gordon is *murdering* my *dolls*!"

Ah Ling came running up. "What for Gordon do this bad thing?" she cried.

Amah seized the guillotine just in time to prevent the executions.

This was a convenient time for reading our store of books, mostly children's encyclopaedias, my Beatrix Potter and a few other books of my brother's. One story I was reading was set in Canada: about a motherless bear cub, taken in as a pet by a boy in the northern wilderness. I loved this tale and longed for a little bear cub of my own.

One afternoon, Ah Fok went shopping and brought in a brown, woolly, bear-like puppy he'd found, with a severe burn on his side, probably made by a hot iron. Amah salved and dressed his wound. We named him Bear.

"Can I keep him Mummy?"

"Yes, dear."

So Amah and I made up a doll's cot with soft rags. Bear slept there by my bed, raised on a chair, until he grew secure enough to join our other dog, Janey, in the kitchen.

Once Bear recovered, he became very much my brother's dog, both of them full of the same mischievous rough-and-tumble zest for life. Bear would pounce on anyone unwary enough not to notice he was there. He bounded after my brother and chased the balls he threw. Bear romped joyfully round the garden that whole long, glorious summer.

Our little cairn terrier, Janey, was lively and kind. She was always very aware of my feelings and came to lick my hand and comfort me in all my childhood troubles. Janey was born to be a mother and later that summer she became pregnant by a dachshund from next door.

We made careful preparations for the arrival of the new puppies. Ah Ling made a large comfortable bed in the kitchen from a box and lined it with old clean blankets and soft sheets. We watched Janey's health and feeding and kept her close to home. Suddenly, however, she disappeared. For over a week we searched the village. Ah Ling left food outside for her.

About two weeks after the disappearance, Ah Ling saw Janey in the garden with a puppy, which she seemed to be trying to shepherd under the kitchen steps. Our amah ran up. With the puppy in her apron and Janey following anxiously behind, Amah came to the bed we had prepared in the kitchen. To add to the comfort of the animals, Gordon had raised the bed and had it swinging on one of his Meccano contraptions. Once Amah had dissuaded Gordon, pointing out a swinging bed merely added anxiety, she fed Janey, and there the dog and puppy both stayed back home with us.

Ah Ling went out to look under the kitchen steps. There she found three more puppies, but they had died. There was an open drain running under the steps and there had not been enough dry space for all the litter.

Then began the amazing last chapter in Janey's life, her life as a mother. She played with and guarded her puppy carefully. Each evening Janey ventured out in the street with it, always accompanied by the dachshund. The two older dogs, with the young one between them, walked along the village road and came back to return him carefully to his home. I shall always remember the poignant sight of the two little dogs with a tiny one between, walking together along the dusty village street.

10. Country Experiences

During an exploring expedition Amah took me to the burial ground for a nearby farm and village. We stood next to the graves, bending to see them better. Here tiny houses about two or three feet high, with red tiled roofs, stood in rows like a miniature town. I asked Ah Ling who lived in such small dwellings, and she said it was the ancestors of the villagers and farmers. Outside the houses there were flowers, and mirrors to ward off evil spirits. To me, the idea of being near one's ancestors, who lived close by in little houses, seemed a very comforting one. I had never met my grandparents, who all died before I was born; neither had I met my aunts and uncles.

This reminded me of another funeral building I'd seen with Amah when we lived in Bubbling Well Road. One day, Ah Ling told me we were going to play in a large garden nearby, owned by a family called the Sassoons. They were from an East Indian trading family, and owned large sections of land in the Settlement. They became very wealthy in India, China and Britain and formed part of the international mosaic of Shanghai.

Amah pushed me in my pram to an enormous walled garden. As we entered the wrought iron gates, I looked along the brick wall and it seemed to run for miles to the horizon. The garden was mainly dense groves of tall trees divided by paved roadways. There were no other people about and no large stretches of grass.

We went along the long roadway meeting no one and I felt scared. At the intersection of two paths we saw a larger than life bronze statue of a seated man, in a formal European suit, set in a clearing.

"Who is that?" I asked,

"He one of Sassoon family. He die."

Rambling around, we came to a small house-like structure, built in the Chinese style, with lights on, mirrors and a little padded bench to sit on. I sat on the bench, looked into the lighted mirrors and asked, "Whose house is this?"

"It belong person who die. It to remember her."

The house was a full-sized structure, much bigger than the little houses for ancestors of country people.

"But *why* is it here in this garden?"

"She good friend of people in house."

The whole effect of the tall densely packed trees and the lack of open space and of other people, the little house and the bronze statue was one of gloom, isolation and sadness. I think Ah Ling felt this too. We never returned to the Sassoon estate. But in my adult life I can't help wondering what a Chinese memorial house for the dead was doing in the garden of an East Indian: a favourite servant perhaps, or a mistress?

My days in the village were full. Michael West was a friend from our compound in Bubbling Well Road. In a typical day's play the two of us spent leisurely hours roaming around, sometimes observing a neighbouring farm.

"What shall we do after we visit the goats?" said Michael.

The baby goat butted my hands with his rounded stubs of horns and the Sikh herdsman gently urged him in with the others. The Sikh's height, emphasized by his turban, made him a giant to my six-year-old eyes. This, my first long stay in the country, gave me a life-long love of green spaces, plants, animals and wildlife – and exhilarating memories of a child's first freedom to roam.

Part of our daily routine was to take some time with the Sikh and his herd of goats. Some of the goats wore bells, and their chiming told us where the grazing ground was for the day. The Sikh accepted our visits, and we watched him milking the animals. The baby goats were tremendous fun to play with. As well as running and charging us, they sprang straight up into the air and dashed about very quickly, like all the very young, before lying down again, exhausted.

"Go and swing," I said running off to our favourite swing, which hung on a tree branch in another garden. We swooped back and forth energetically, high into the leafy green of the tree. A nest of wasps, that also occupied the branch, added a delicious sense of danger. The wasps came and went, buzzing and determined on their summer's work. They didn't seem to notice the tremor caused by our swinging.

"Let's go to your house," said Michael.

Our main aim on the way to each other's houses was not to touch the ground. We walked along the tops of all the garden walls. A major obstacle on each house front along our route was the iron garden gate. If the gate was closed, our crossing was easy; we swung across by the ornamental iron spikes. An open gate meant a more complicated manoeuvre. This time Michael had to swing on the gate until it closed and we could continue.

For variety, we left the wall to see how far we could progress along the trees in the front gardens before we had to return to the wall and continue along it. In this way we completed our journey to my house, and let ourselves in by swinging off a tree. One jump and we were in the side garden. There we could play and have picnics, provisioned with sandwiches, lemonade and cakes by Ah Fok and Ah Ling.

The undergrowth provided splendid cover for hide and seek and ball throwing or pouncing games with Bear. The hide and seek tended to be a waste of time, if Bear gave away our hiding places. When he was outside, we went into a ball throwing and rolling-around-with-Bear mode.

We caught grasshoppers, put them in a large matchbox with air holes so they could breathe, took them for a ride on our bikes and then returned them to freedom. A previous hunt for the insects almost ended in disaster. I went out by myself and ran around following a particularly large and lively grasshopper all over the front garden. I was just about to catch it when my father swooped me up away from the "grasshopper" which he explained was really a praying mantis. We watched it for a while and my father told me about the praying mantis. People thought it gave a painful sting.

In our daily wanderings, Michael and I watched the farmers. Their straw hats firmly tied on with string, they carefully fertilized each plant with the local sewage and the manure from the farm's livestock. Nothing was wasted. There was no mechanization, and all work was done by the farm's animals and their owners.

Watching a cow or a donkey walking round and round turning a stone quern to grind flour was to prove a useful learning experience for the future. The grain was put into a hole running down through the middle of a large, round stone. It was ground into flour that collected in a trough hollowed out around the edge of the lower stone. Through a chute carved into the side of the trough, a farm labourer brushed the flour into a container from where it went to the market for sale or to the house for use in cooking or baking.

As we watched the grinding of millet in particular, we were interested to learn that flour is not only white but yellow as well. So far we had seen white and whole wheat flour only. We had facetious discussions about what you would bake with yellow flour.

"Sunshine cake," said Michael.

"Maybe Daffodil cake," I guessed.

The relative freedom allowed by country life perfectly suited Gordon's fearless, adventurous nature. Behind the village's main street lived an elderly Chinese who grew sugar cane in the field beside his house. Raw sugar cane, fresh from the nearby market, was delightful. We sucked the sweet juice and threw away the fibrous remains.

On one of the long warm summer evenings, when all the children gathered after dinner, Gordon and his friends were looking for some excitement with the spice of danger.

"Let's go and steal some sugar cane," someone said.

"Yes, let's. Let's."

All the bigger children ran to the farmer's field, and I tagged along. Quietly we slid between the stalks, which rustled as we passed. They were about three times as high as I was. Someone giggled. The farmer was vigilant, and came out of his house waving a long stick and shouting at us in Chinese. He was really angry.

Everyone ran away empty-handed. As we ran I suddenly found myself left far behind, firmly stuck in mud. I couldn't pull my feet from the heavy wet soil.

Oh no, the farmer will kill me, I wailed to myself. "Gordon, help me!" I yelled.

The farmer, brandishing his cane, bore down on us as I screamed in terror.

Maybe this is a nightmare and I'll wake up, I thought.

Just in time my brother returned, pulled me out minus a sandal, and rushed me home.

Amah started: "What for you do this bad thing?" she said to us both, shaking her head at our muddy state. Then gently and patiently Amah bathed us and put on our light summer pyjamas. She tucked in the mosquito netting and turned off the light. Safety, calmness, sleep…. The "excitement" of trying to steal sugar cane may have appealed to my brother and his friends, but it was not to my taste.

In the country I also became aware for the first time of the nocturnal life of the area. Very early in the morning, I would often wake up briefly to hear the slap of bare feet and subdued conversation in Chinese.

The first time I heard this, I peered out of the screened veranda where I slept and saw coolies outlined against the moonlight on the village road. Each carried two large containers (nicknamed honey pots by Britishers) at either end of a bamboo pole slung over one shoulder. The containers held the night soil from the city and nearby villages, carefully collected and now being taken past our house to fertilize the vegetables growing in the neighbouring farmlands.

As I lay in my bed on the veranda overlooking the street, I imagined the carriers in their black clothes and bare feet, taking the containers to the farm people we saw during the day. They formed a comforting domestic interlude in the night

11. Rough Winds

The summer dawdled along and we experienced the full heat and oppressive humidity of the local climate; Shanghai was built on marshy ground. Our mothers watched carefully to make sure we children always wore our floppy cotton sun hats when we left the house.

During this village stay, as the heat and humidity increased, I often thought of the Race Course swimming club, where before the occupation we had spent the whole day in hot weather with our friends. We ran about and swam, ate hot dogs and drank Coca Cola (like American children) to keep us going until we returned home for dinner. If we wanted we could have tiffin in the clubhouse.

By the time I was two years old I could get around in water by dog paddling. At the age of three or four I entered a swimming competition. It was for under-fives to swim a breadth of the pool. At the shout of "Go!" I jumped off the edge of the swimming pool with a horde of others and, urged on by my brother, paddled furiously for the other side. Gordon then ran to the end of the course and, putting his hands down in the water, yelled at me to come quickly.

With encouragement like that I couldn't help being the first to reach the end of the race and be pulled out by him.

As a prize, I received a silver napkin ring with my initials engraved on it. My mother put it in the china cabinet.

As the humidity became worse, everyone in the village made good use of ceiling and hand-held fans. We put on our light summer pyjamas and tucked mosquito nets (suspended from the ceiling) round our beds while Amah sprayed Flit. We talked together about our summers before the war. Previously, after school ended, women and children had made a mass exit to the seaside for a two-month summer holiday. Sometimes we went to stay in a hotel in north China at Wei Hai Wei (Way-High-Way), which had a stunning, sandy beach and always produced glorious weather – or Obama where there were hot sulphur springs, or to the seaside village of Katsusa in Japan.

I thought about the excitement of going on our summer break. Before we went, there was a flurry of packing and hanging clothes in steamer trunks with drawers for underwear and toys, and coat hangers for longer garments. Whatever our destination, the holiday always started with a trip on an ocean liner. The ships seemed enormous to us as children. They were coal-fired, and when we boarded we saw swarms of coolies carrying bags of coal to the cargo gangway, still refuelling for the journey. We had our own suite of rooms and away we went, past the Bund down the Whangpoo and Yangtze to the sea. I had something of a problem as, with the slightest swell, I was seasick, even on the Yangtze if it was a bit choppy.

On a trip to Japan from Shanghai, for two days (out of the five) the sea was yellowy brown, before changing to the normal shade of blue-green. This colour comes from mud from the mighty Yangtze, which flows 4,000 miles from its source in the highlands of Tibet to the 200-mile wide estuary.

Ah Ling accompanied us for the whole holiday, and Ah Fok would remain to look after our pets and my father who joined us for only part of our stay. There were many activities provided for all ages. Deck quoits and movies were favourites.

Meals were a very formal affair for which we dressed. There were no play clothes allowed here. If you put your knife and fork together (indicating you'd finished eating) instead of crossed (to indicate you were continuing) a waiter would whisk away the plate.

The pervasive continuous hum of the engines, which gave a cozy feeling of being in a little secure world of one's own, was one of the pleasures of travelling by ship. And I also enjoyed going to the boat deck to watch the hypnotic writhing of the ship's wake, endlessly curling in light green and white ribbons into the horizon.

In the late 1930s, when we were travelling to our holiday destinations, the sea was still teeming with marine life. Whales spouted in the distance, schools of porpoises routinely accompanied us for miles; and we could see enormous jellyfish, about eight feet across, moving along by contracting and expanding themselves.

All these thoughts and discussions of our previous summers led us to ask our parents whether they would think of some way we could play in water despite being confined to the village. There was a large, concrete back-up water tank behind the Japanese headquarters and some of the parents asked if it could be filled with water for swimming. The Japanese not only agreed but also provided a guard to make sure no one drowned.

And so every afternoon for the balance of the hot weather, we went to swim and play in the tank, watched over by a Japanese soldier at attention. The tank was a fraction of the size of the swimming club pool but we thoroughly enjoyed ourselves. As usual my brother and his friends fooled around splashing everyone else. We didn't speak much Japanese and were not able to talk to the soldiers who stood on guard.

But there was a change in behaviour from the extremely indulgent attitude towards children characteristic of our summer holidays in Japan. Somehow, despite the concession to our comfort, friendly chat didn't seem to be appropriate and the soldiers never smiled when watching over us but stood to attention, bayonets fixed. When we played around the village the Japanese military personnel, with their bayonets and staccato shouting, were distant. Here at the swimming tank they were close, and observably grim.

Still I found it hard to imagine the Japanese doing something terrible. Instead, I daydreamed about a perfect day on a holiday to Japan ...

We rise from the floor where we've been sleeping on soft futons, and roll them up for storage during the day in a cupboard. These cloth sleeping mats were about two inches thick, not to be confused with the tatami floor coverings that are very firm and covered in a shiny, smooth woven natural material, like very fine basket weave, attached to boards.

After breakfast Ah Ling takes me round to see her friends the shopkeepers in the village of Katsusa in the southern Japanese region of Shimabara. They bow and compliment Amah about me, and give sweets wrapped in rice paper. We walk along the main street where Japanese families greet us in soft, polite voices. Unlike in the cities, here they have not adopted western dress. Gracefully attired in kimonos, the mother and girls always walk behind the father and boys. Amah and I try to return the courteous bows with a little obeisance of our own. Amah says we must bend at the hips not the waist.

That afternoon after tiffin a woman, bare to the waist, comes to the back door with baskets of live crabs on either end of a carrying pole. Amah chooses which one to have for dinner by putting it on the kitchen table to see it walk around. After she has seen several crabs, Amah points to the most lively one, and the vendor continues to the next house.

In the early evening we sit outside and talk in the drifting smoke from slow-burning scented coils that deter insects. We take finely chopped meat to feed to an enormous toad, the size of a dinner plate, which emerges to see us, sitting quietly to one side. He is our pet for the summer.

That evening everyone, except Amah and me, goes to a place referred to as The Hotel. Despite my pleading, I am always left behind because I am too young. Then Ah Ling takes me to visit a Japanese family whose house also overlooks the beach. The Japanese greet us ceremoniously with many bows. They pass tea and different kinds of little cakes, fruit and sweets from person to person. The adults don't ignore me but treat me with great kindness and respect. I think I am the lucky one. It is a wonderful way to end the day.

When the sun is setting, the men remove one side of the room overlooking the sea and we enjoy the glorious sunset. As we talk quietly, the bright colours of the evening sky gradually darken to blend in with the sea. This is a holy time. The family calls this their sunset-viewing room.

Then we move to another room where we lounge on futons and eat more little cakes with tea. This time the men have removed part of the ceiling and I gaze up at the black velvet sky with its millions of stars. We never see this in the city, but with no lights on outside, the stars shine out quite clearly. They seem so near that I could stretch out my hand and pick a few.

After a while we all lie with our heads on hard rolled pillows. There is a kind of ringing silence. I wonder whether we're supposed to go to sleep, and sneak a look at the others. But no, they're still looking at the sky. I look back up. And then it happens; sailing slowly across our window in the ceiling comes the large yellow lantern of the moon.

There is a collective, soft "Ahhh ..."

PART II
CAPTIVITY

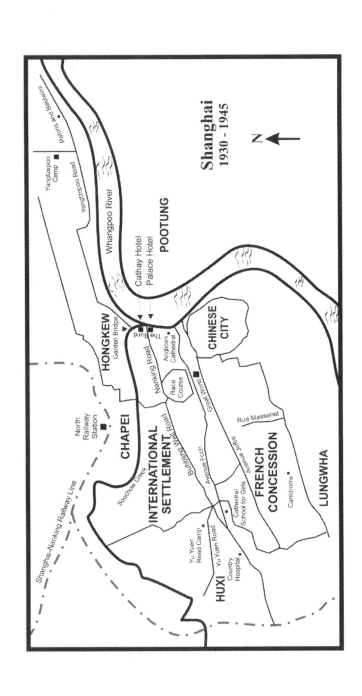

12. Separations

As the summer ended, our parents heard rumours of internment camps being set up, and that certain community leaders would be imprisoned first. The village families made a heart-wrenching decision about their pets. One morning a Portuguese doctor came and gave a lethal injection to each animal and bird. The vets in Shanghai, sickened of this task, had been unable to continue. My mother explained we would be going away again, where we would not be able to keep our pets. They could not look after themselves, and it was better to give them a painless death.

Parents dug a grave behind our house, and there was a burial ceremony. Very slowly and reverently the other children of the village, walking in single file, carried their dead pets, and laid them gently down in the earth, which was lined with sheets. The adults carefully folded the sheets over the dead animals and birds, and filled in the open grave. The children sang a hymn, "All Things Bright and Beautiful", in benediction and farewell.

Gardens were blossoming in their last glorious burst before the winter, and to complete the ceremony the children picked whatever they wanted. They came and went until they transformed the muddy grave into a mound of brilliant flowers.

I did not take part directly in this ceremony. In tears I watched from inside the house as my brother slowly followed the others in procession and carried the small bodies of our dogs to their grave. I thought of curling up in a chair with Janey, of seeing Janey with her puppy, and playing with Bear. It was hard to grasp that I would never again see them. Our dogs were so alive, and then suddenly not alive. I thought that surely this dreadful thing could be undone and they would come to see us again. I had never felt that sense of loss, never cried like that before.

A few days after the burial of our pets a loud crash jolted Gordon and me awake in the evening. Several Japanese soldiers kicked in the front door and entered, running with noisy boots up the stairs, shouting, guns drawn. The leading soldier pointed a gun at my father's chest and interrogated him through an interpreter. I made the mistake of going forward to smile and say hello to the soldiers. *Surely if I'm nice to them they will turn back to being like the Japanese we met on holiday, and stop threatening my father,* I thought. Amah quickly took me out of harm's way. My father kept very calm and showed no fear, neither did he make any sudden movements.

The other soldiers searched the whole house. They turned out all the drawers and other containers onto the floors and threatened us with their weapons. My mother put her hand to the side of her face, a habit she had when upset. As abruptly as they came, the soldiers decided to depart, leaving our family to clear up the mess late into the night with the help of Ah Fok and Ah Ling.

"*Why* are the soldiers so angry with Daddy?"

"Don't worry dear, they didn't hurt us."

My mother rushed to put away her private belongings thrown out in full view on the floor. I remember a corset and other underclothes. Gordon and I had to gather up all our own garments, books and toys, and help put back any salvageable food items. We washed cutlery before putting it back into drawers, then huddled together for comfort. Eventually Ah Fok cleaned the last spills and we all went back to bed.

We did not discuss this incident further, but it was a warning of the danger we faced. I felt afraid.

Two days later, my parents told me they needed to prepare for the next move in our lives. They said we'd be going to live in a smaller amount of space than we had now, and that they would be deciding what to take and what to leave behind. I would have a better time spending a few days visiting our friends the Lewises at Patons and Baldwins, a nearby manufacturing company.

Amah and my mother spent time packing a bag with my clothes and favourite toys. The blue giraffe was too big for the little suitcase and so I hugged his soft body in my arms. The giraffe's head hung over my shoulder. My father drew a picture of me on a swing in the Patons and Baldwins playground, to take on my visit. Mrs. Lewis came in a rickshaw and I boarded it with many hugs from my mother and Amah, and an especially long hug from my father. He seemed sad that day, as he answered my goodbye wave with one of his own. I felt the same, knowing I'd miss him and our lessons together, even for just a little while.

Neilson Lewis, his wife Rhoda and daughter Kathleen (Kay) lived in the Patons and Baldwins company compound where Neilson was in charge of the dye house. Patons and Baldwins produced knitting wool. The compound, just outside Shanghai, was divided into an area for houses, set in spacious lawns, a park with a children's playground, and a factory area with high walls and spaces between the buildings paved in concrete. There was also the clubhouse where we could have lunch.

Patons and Baldwins had a macabre fame because of its location near a bend in the Whangpoo river where, in a quirk of current, bodies of those drowned or "buried" in the river washed up and had to be pushed off again with long poles to continue their slow journey to the sea.

Mrs. Lewis was very motherly. She helped me to dress when I woke up, and Uncle Neilson read a story at bedtime. *How long will I be staying here? I can't ask the Lewises, it would be bad manners. They are so kind, yet I want to go home.*

In the mornings I put on my dungarees and sweater and went out to the factory area to roller-skate using skates borrowed from Kathleen, who was away at the Cathedral Girls' School all week. She stayed in Shanghai with some friends and came back at the weekend.

In the afternoons I avidly read Kathleen's books, by Joyce Lankester Brisley, about Milly-Molly-Mandy, a little dark-haired girl who lived in an English village with her large extended family. The family members all looked alike, being rounded, dark-haired and very cheerful. The little girl helped her grandmother to bake, or her father to do the garden, or her aunt to prepare for a village fete. Milly-Molly-Mandy's lively adventures in her English village distracted me from the troubles looming in my own life.

During our stay in Ningkuo Road, after the summer, my brother Gordon had a harder life than either Kathleen or myself. He made the over one-hour journey to the Cathedral Boys' School by bicycle. There was another school nearby, but my parents thought it better for Gordon to attend the one he was accustomed to. It seemed sensible for me to continue working with my father, as the work was basic, and the task was pleasant for both of us.

Gordon got up at half past six o'clock to begin his long journey by seven after a breakfast of porridge with Tate and Lyle syrup, a boiled egg and toast. He always made a lake of the syrup in the middle of the porridge. Gordon had lunch at school and returned at around 6:00 p.m. for dinner, with homework still to complete. When he arrived home he left his bicycle outside for Ah Fok to put away in the garage behind the house. Then my brother limped upstairs with his school satchel. Gordon's injured leg was always stiff after the long ride. Ah Fok served dinner as soon as possible after my brother came, and then quickly cleared the table so that Gordon could do his homework there, helped by our father. Bedtime on weekdays was half past eight, and Gordon was usually fast asleep within minutes.

On my first weekend with the Lewises Kathleen returned and I had someone to play with. Then on November 6 during the following week, at last, the time came for my return. I rushed in to see my father again. I couldn't find him.

"Where's Daddy?" I asked my mother. She hugged me, but seemed sad.

"The Japanese have taken him."

"When? When will he come back?"

"I don't know. They took him away early yesterday morning."

"*Where?*"

"To a prison at Haiphong Road, quite near Bubbling Well Road."

"*Why?*"

"It's for political prisoners of the Japanese."

"Will he be all right?"

"I believe so. Don't worry dear."

My mother may have told me not to worry, but she was plainly worried and upset herself. She didn't seem able to continue answering my questions. So Amah came and took me to the kitchen where she sat me on her knee and hugged me for a long time.

After the invasion and search of our house, my parents realized my father would soon be arrested. They sent me away as they thought it would be better for me not to see him taken by soldiers.

Later I asked, "Will Daddy be sad all the time in his prison? Will we see him again soon?" questions no one could answer.

"Will Daddy be able to draw and paint?" My mother told me he had taken his art supplies with him. In fact on that first Christmas without my father I had proof that he had his art supplies, when we received a hand-made Christmas card with a joyful message and a drawing of Santa Claus.

Aunt Haruko and Uncle Steve Wilkinson, good friends of our parents, invited us to spend the holiday with them, and despite the shadow of our father's absence, we had a wonderful time. My present was an enormous baby doll, and Gordon's was a flashlight, with a magnifying lens in front. He woke me up early as usual on Christmas morning, shining light on the ceiling, making a huge yellow circle with it.

During our stay with the Wilkinsons, Gordon started stirring his evening cocoa quickly round and round forming a little whirlpool that almost, but not quite, overflowed onto the tablecloth. Aunt Haruko looked upset and I could see our mother was annoyed. Once he realized how well he was literally stirring things up, he did this with any liquid he was drinking until told to stop by our exasperated parent.

The rest of our stay in the village was full of foreboding. Japanese were preparing internment camps for all Allied civilians but the British Residents' Association took over the actual assignment of prisoners, to provide a balance of people with particular skills in each camp. Then in the Anglo-Chinese Treaty of January 11, 1943, the British government gave away to the Chinese Nationalists all the assets and liabilities of the Shanghai Municipal Council and renounced all the extra-territorial rights (extrality) of British subjects in China. These rights gave the British the protection of their own laws within the International Settlement, although they still had to obey the Land Regulations.

I asked my mother to explain the internment camp

where we'd be living. She took Gordon and me to the kitchen at the back of our apartment.

"We may only have the size of this kitchen for our living space," she said

"Do you mean to sleep?" asked Gordon.

"No, for everything."

"Will we have a kitchen in it like this?" I asked.

"I'm afraid not. We'll probably all have to line up for food at one big kitchen. That's why we're taking enamel plates, mugs and bowls. They won't break if we drop them. There should be some bathrooms that everyone will use. We'll find out how things work when we get there."

"Maybe we could take futons and roll them up after we're awake like we did in Japan," I said.

"It could be cold sleeping on the floor in winter," said my mother. "I'll have three beds for us."

"Can I take my own special bed?"

"It's becoming too small for you dear, so I'm buying you an adult one."

With that Gordon and I had to be satisfied, as we started to prepare for our internment, deciding what things we could carry ourselves. I felt excited at the responsibility of choosing my own things to take, and having a grown-up bed, although I would miss my bed carved with Mickey Mouse and his friends. *Surely everything will be all right with Mummy there to look after us,* I thought. With deep regret we had to leave behind most books, and the large doll given to me the previous Christmas.

Finally I chose my teddy bear, my beloved baby doll, the blue stuffed giraffe, a Beatrix Potter book about Jeremy Fisher, the first volume of the Children's Encyclopedia

(A-D) and *The Golden Book of Wonder* containing a large collection of beautifully illustrated children's poems and stories from around the world, actually belonging to my brother. The paper was very fine, strong and thin; the publisher, Odhams Press, had been able to pack a lot of reading into relatively little space. I added a blank notebook and some pencils with a pencil sharpener.

Helped by Ah Fok and Ah Ling, we packed away all our other belongings.

"Why are we putting away things we can't take with us?"

"We're getting them ready to be used by the Japanese families of the village soldiers, who'll be moving in when we leave."

Outside each box we pasted a list of what was inside. My mother had warm, practical clothes made for all of us by one of the many excellent tailors for which China is well known and bought herself a third single bed. For a week or two we camped in the flat with just enough to see us through until the day when we had to leave.

"Can we dig up Janey and Puppy and Bear and take them with us?" I asked

"I'm afraid not. They have to stay here."

We asked Ah Fok and Ah Ling what they would do after we left. Ah Fok said he would go to his family in central Shanghai. Ah Ling decided to return to her own people in Canton.

Soon we knew when we had to go, and where: to the Yu Yuen Road camp at the other end of Shanghai. For one last time, Amah put me to bed. Putting her hands round either side of my head (a wonderful feeling) she whispered, "Margaret go sleep well." In the morning, Amah washed and dressed me, gently brushed my hair and gave me breakfast. I had lost our pets and my father, now I was to lose Ah Ling, my Chinese mother.

Not long after breakfast, lorries drew up outside and male European prisoners loaded our heavier belongings. To take us with our lighter baggage, we called a pedicab. It was a cross between a tricycle and a rickshaw, which allowed the coolie to pedal seated passengers around instead of having to run between the shafts pulling them. After one last hug from Ah Ling, we climbed on and went back across Soochow Creek, then past Bubbling Well Road, and so to our first internment camp in Yu Yuen Road, just inside the Settlement's boundary with the old Outside Roads, the Badlands.

As we crossed the towering metal framework of the Garden Bridge a tram went before us. At the Japanese checkpoint the driver leaned out to bow and give the mandatory polite greeting about the Emperor in fractured Japanese. The passengers and the pedicab driver concealed grins. When we were going along the middle of the bridge our driver told us that, in Chinese, the "greeting" the Chinese tram driver managed to give, twisting the Japanese words a bit, was very rude indeed (in the Chinese language).

Japanese soldiers were driving Chinese pedestrians through the checkpoint with their rifle butts.

"Mummy *why* are the Japanese always so horrible to the Chinese?"

"They don't respect them. The Japanese don't even think of the Chinese as human beings like themselves."

As we left the bridge the pedicab slowed down to avoid the bright green sparks thrown by the tram from the suspended overhead cable. I shrank back. I thought, *We don't have the sides of a car to protect us now.* I felt tired, shivery and alone, isolated in the pedicab, as if I hadn't been asleep the night before, as if I didn't have a place in which to sleep tonight. Japanese people were living in our house in Bubbling Well Road and soon others would live in the village flat as well. I couldn't go back home any more.

13. Bitter Sauces

It is early morning in Katsusa. The sky is cornflower blue, the sand like fine brown sugar. Sunlight folds us in a comforting warmth – and we can see for miles …

Waves curl slowly along the shore and fishermen plod by with their night's catch in baskets slung on either end of the bamboo poles across their shoulders. In the light breeze we catch a whiff of the fish, still salty from the sea.

After breakfast in the kitchen with Amah, Gordon and I are going to visit our friend next door. He takes us in to watch his uncle, meditating cross-legged on a low platform. The boys start pulling faces and jumping up and down. The man's serene inward gaze ignores them.

But suddenly he springs up and chases us shouting. His voice becomes louder … and I jerk starkly awake, to the sound and feel of my mother slammed back across my bed, propelled by blows from a drunken Japanese guard.

His loud, enraged staccato creates a harsh discord with the frantic cries of our neighbour Mrs. Sanbrook, who is begging her husband not to strike the guard, and with my mother's groans. In the random flashes from the guard's torch as he waves it about, our bleak room, with its bare walls and worn wood floor, springs haphazardly into focus like some grim jigsaw puzzle. I see the peeling paint of the ceiling with no light bulb, the small metal table where we eat, my yellow teddy bear, blue giraffe, baby doll and well-thumbed books on the floor, the other two beds (for my mother and brother) and the curved sword and drawn gun of the guard's companion. I wonder whether he is going to shoot, or cut us to pieces.

We share a partitioned room with the Sanbrooks. Mrs. Sanbrook is already awake and standing to attention with her husband and two young sons. She quietly urges us to get up and stand in a row bowing from the hips. We all do as she says. The guard gives another enraged shout at our bowed heads but does not attack anyone again. He goes out to the corridor to continue his roll call.

We wait in our rooms, keeping very quiet, fearful the guards will come back; but after what seems like a long time we hear them stamping up the stone stairs opposite our room to take roll call on the floor above. We wait another age until we hear the guards clattering back down to leave the building.

Then my mother tells us to go back to sleep and she feels her way along the corridor in the dark to the room with two lavatories and a row of washbasins. There she bathes in cold water to reduce the swelling and bruises that are coming up on the side of her face and body. Our mother washes and washes herself. Over and over the cleaning continues. Can she ever wash away the experience?

My brother and I sit up.

"Where is she now?" I whisper.

"She'll come soon."

"But *when?*"

"Go to sleep."

At last we hear her cautious steps, the creak of the door as she quietly opens and shuts it behind her. At *last* our mother is back. We both pretend we've been asleep all the time, but after a while I hear my mother whisper, "Alex, Alex." I slip into my mother's bed and hug her. Soon we all do fall asleep and it is daytime. The bell rings for our morning roll call and congee breakfast. Things are back to normal.

For several weeks we had lived in the Shanghai Municipal Council's Western District Public School, a solid brick building called B-Block, beside the Public School for Girls, called G-Block. Some wooden huts behind the playing field were labelled T-Camp because they backed onto Tifeng Road. Separated from each other by grass playing fields bordered by trees, the former schools were on Shanghai's Yu Yuen Road. This was not the gracious environment of sweeping oak staircases, panelled walls, tennis courts and flower gardens I knew at the Cathedral Girls' School, and yet I was later to regard this first camp as our luxury internment camp.

The school's classrooms were all divided into two, each part allocated to a family. We occupied part of a corner room, which we entered from the main corridor through a door to a small hallway. Doors led from this hallway to the half rooms occupied by our family and the Sanbrooks with their two sons. Because of the insulation of the two doors, we had slept through a bell for the extra roll call at 2 a.m.

Mrs. Sanbrook was a kind, frail-looking woman with pale hair, and was complemented by her husband, Jack; a tall, fair, cheerful man, he spent his spare time lifting weights. Their sons were about seven and four years old. The older boy, John, was like his mother, and the younger one, Georgie, took after his father.

My mother's bruises healed in a week or two and, at least in the sense of the physical injuries, this was the end of that particular incident. It was not the end of being woken up in the middle of the night. Depriving their prisoners of sleep was one of the ways the Japanese used to torment and demoralize us. From then on we left our door to the corridor open at night. At first these extra roll calls caused a long spell of wakefulness, but after a few months we became accustomed to stumbling up and then falling quickly back to sleep.

Sleeping, or rather waking up, became a potentially embarrassing experience for me as, like several other children, I began to wet my bed. I was almost seven and felt too old for this. I was fortunate, as unlike some others, my mother never scolded, she simply said not to worry, sponged the mattress and put it across the windowsill to dry in the sun.

Just as we children changed in response to the new circumstances, some adults also altered their behaviour. Within a few weeks of entering our camp Mrs. Smith, who lived two rooms away from ours, began to wash her hands constantly. She insisted that her daughter Mary should do the same. We often saw them at the school's washbasins. Mary seemed very anxious. After a while, Mrs. Smith went to be cared for at a psychiatric hospital until the end of the war.

Aunt Haruko also changed. She had been a smiling, bubbly person, but became fearful of what would happen to us, with good reason: having a Japanese mother, she knew more about their culture than we did. To the Japanese we were people whom they despised for allowing themselves to be taken prisoner in the first place, and their response could be very violent. As the Allied forces were to discover when they invaded Japanese territory such as the islands of Saipan and Iwo Jima, the Japanese civilian reaction to the threat of capture was to kill their children and themselves to avoid the "loss of face" involved in being defeated. The army's soldiers urged them on, to show the superiority of the Japanese race.

The new conditions inspired some people to be more ingenious than they had needed to be before they entered the camp. On the same (second) floor of the 3-storey B-Block as us lived the Duncans with their daughter Sheila, about ten, and their young son Peter, about four years old. Sheila was a fine-boned, coltish girl with flaming red, tightly wavy hair, Katherine Hepburn-ish. She danced wonderfully in concerts given by the class in modern dancing held by parents. Her little brother Peter was always in mischief of some sort. There was a general ripple of concern along our floor when Peter bit off and swallowed part of a glass thermometer while the camp doctor, also a prisoner, was taking his temperature. He prescribed an immediate sandwich of cotton wool, and this caused a hasty general search. A large cotton wool "meal" saved the boy from internal cuts.

Early during our imprisonment Mr. Kawasaki, the camp commandant, asked for help from the prisoners in mending his old radio, which tended to break down. He wanted to keep it, as he liked the cabinet the radio was in.

The electrician who responded, from time to time asked for more extra parts than he needed. After a while, he had enough to make another, short wave, radio to obtain news of the war.

The electrician disguised it as his child's pull toy, a truck, which when not in use was sometimes left in full view being played with by his son. The place for plugging in and listening to the radio was behind a small dummy wall near the G-Block kitchen, where a map of the world was also kept. The Japanese were never able to discover how we knew what was happening in the world outside.

For the rest of the conflict a few men, alternating, listened at night in secret, covered in a "tent" of blankets to deaden the sound. They could receive Australian stations as well as KGEI in San Francisco. Although the guards generally patrolled only around the camp walls, other prisoners acted as look-outs in case a guard should happen to decide to come into the camp itself. This they sometimes did, but usually after ringing a bell for an extra, nighttime roll call. So during the later war years the prisoners passed on to each other by word-of-mouth news of how the Allies were progressing.

14. Spring

Soon the adults arranged a camp administration, which was a committee of men. The one with the highest profile, Mr. Henry (Harry) Robertson, conducted any negotiations necessary with the camp commandant. He had been a deputy commissioner of the Shanghai Municipal Police, and was voted into his position at Yu Yuen Road by the internees casting ballots in two groups: Shanghai Municipal Council employees, and businessmen. (Wives voted with their husband's category.) In this way, the camp set up the *Pao Chia* system imposed outside, with a man in charge of the good behaviour of a set or sets of other people. Harry Robertson was responsible for the good behaviour of the whole camp.

Mr. Robertson was over six feet tall, always immaculately dressed and spoke with an educated Scottish accent. He had greying fair hair and was about ten years older than my father. The prisoners thought Mr. Robertson's impenetrable calmness and superior negotiating skills helped save many tense situations.

The internees also decided on an interpreter. The obvious and best one to choose was Aunt Haruko but such was the distrust, given that her mother was Japanese, that they chose someone else who was not as competent in Japanese as Aunt Haruko, and the adults suspected we did not have good translations. There was some mutual puzzlement in dealings between the Japanese and the prisoners. However, they persevered with their choice of interpreter, and managed.

The first commandant was Mr. Kawasaki, an old-style diplomat from the Japanese consulate in Shanghai. He was in his sixties and had a very distinguished bearing. Mr. Kawasaki brought in the consular police as the major part of our guards. On our first day in the camp he ordered all the prisoners to gather together on the B-Block playing field. Between the playing areas behind the former Girls' and Boys' schools, and raised above the level of the spring flood, was a path on which Mr. Kawasaki stood.

I looked up at the Commandant who was flanked by two of his senior officials. Mr. Kawasaki looked old. He seemed totally alone. I wondered whether he had a wife and children. (We found out he was happily married for over twenty years to an American lady. When the war with the United States started Mr. Kawasaki had to divorce his wife who returned to her homeland. They had no children. The cabinet containing his radio was probably a memento of his marriage.) Mr. Kawasaki sternly told us we were now prisoners of the Japanese Empire, which would last forever. He said we would never again return to our previous lives, or see the homes we had just left. I did not believe Mr. Kawasaki.

Our commandant noticed Aunt Haruko's Japanese name and asked her to come and see him. They conversed in Imperial Japanese, a very formal, polite form of the language used at court. He showed her the passports, which gave her nationality as British and Belgian. Her father was a Belgian diplomat and her mother was from a Japanese family of high rank. Mr. Kawasaki said if Aunt Haruko had been pure Japanese he would have allowed her to leave the camp, but as it was, she had to stay. Aunt Haruko replied she would not have left, as she would not abandon her husband.

Mr. Kawasaki was extremely courteous to all the prisoners. However he was moved to another internment camp and another Japanese diplomat, Mr. Hayashi, came to replace him. Mr. Hayashi was younger and had been moved to Yu Yuen Road camp from Lungwha camp because there had been several escapes from there.

At first we children adjusted well to the new circumstances, and regarded going to Yu Yuen Road camp as an adventure. We rushed around finding old friends and making new ones. There was always someone to play with. I couldn't wait to get up at dawn and pester my mother for permission to go out to play before breakfast.

There were endless games of hopscotch and leapfrog, also massive games of kick-the-can and hide-and-seek, in which children of all ages joined. These competitions went on for hours. Marbles became an obsession. My brother started me off with one or two marbles of his own, and I won some and lost some in hard-fought games. We did some spirited trading to balance our marble collections between the more valuable and less valuable types.

I started to feel more in control of my own life than ever before. I learned to wash and dress myself without the help I'd previously had from Amah. Now I was able to roam about without having to report in every few minutes. In a bizarre way we children were safer, on our own in the camp, than we had been before entering its confines. We couldn't wander far and our parents had less need to worry about us. But my mother did warn me not to go near the fence, which the guards patrolled. We had no more school, no more music, dancing and riding lessons, nothing to do but roam around and hone our social and sports skills. We soon settled into our freewheeling daily routine, doing as we pleased.

Overcrowding brought people into close contact. Many adults knew each other already and joined for conversations when they had finished their camp tasks: making food in large amounts for the whole camp, keeping the public places clean, caring for the sick in a sick bay they set up, and generally running the everyday aspects of the place. The children gathered in the same family groups as their parents, and on the whole the internees managed a friendly social life with good company there for anyone who wanted it, and support for those in trouble. Given the walls between family rooms, there was still the opportunity for those who liked a more solitary existence to hide, but they always had their families with them.

During these first few months there were some light-hearted shenanigans. In the beginning the whole camp was tormented by a Japanese boy in a terrace house just outside. Everyone had to listen to him practising the trumpet in the evenings. Our boys began to throw stones over the wall at the other boy's window, distracting him. Some men eventually broke the glass, using a slingshot and a marble. Infuriated the young "musician" yelled in English,

"Who did that?" and before running away one of our boys shouted back "Mickey Mouse." This became known as the Mickey Mouse Affair. It led to severe beating for a prisoner, Frederick Jones, who threw the fatal stone.

The Mickey Mouse affair gave my brother an idea for annoying and defying the Japanese. Gordon collected stones from around the camp and took every opportunity to throw them at the houses opposite, hitting windows. The camp liaison officer, Mr. Robertson, soon found the culprit. Gordon reported to Mr. Robertson's room. He looked at the immaculately dressed, erect figure of the officer with some alarm. Then Gordon received a stern lecture about the danger into which he was putting himself and other prisoners. Mr. Robertson pointed out that so far our commandant was Mr. Kawasaki, but information had come through that another commandant, Mr. Hayashi, would soon take over and may add some soldiers to our guards. He told Gordon that the military reaction to provocation would be very violent and could put all the other people in the camp into danger. Gordon promised to behave, and stopped the defiant actions.

This incident was typical of Gordon. From a very early age he showed a total disregard of danger. My mother told me the story of when he was six years old and the staff of the German Embassy opposite watched in horror as Gordon walked the top of the thin iron railing of the balcony surrounding the tenth floor apartment we occupied before the house in Bubbling Well Road. He wobbled precariously at times then jumped down to the balcony and ran inside. The next day our father had the whole outside of the balcony protected with a wrought iron barrier. From the German Embassy staff my parents discovered that previously Gordon had been leaning far out of a window "fishing" with a string in imitation of Tom Sawyer, hero of the book he had just read.

Occasionally on our seaside holidays we experienced the end of one of the many typhoons (fast, violent storms) that hit the China Sea. Gordon rode like a mythological sea sprite on the top of high waves before swooping down into the trough. He always hated to come in out of the storm and on one of our holidays in Japan when he was five years old this caused him a major injury. Wading out of the sea in the shallows as a typhoon passed, Gordon was picked up by a wave and dashed against a rock. He had no difficulty reaching shore but soon started to complain of severe pain in the leg that had been hit. There was no redness or bruising, but a local doctor diagnosed osteomyelitis, a bone disease not uncommon in Japanese coastal regions where people suffered injuries similar to my brother's.

Our parents rushed Gordon to Shanghai where doctors cut his leg open to the bone from knee to ankle and packed it with some agent to fight the disease. This process involved many, sometimes weekly, operations to keep the wound open and to pick out pieces of infected bone. Gordon was brave about the repeated operations. The whole treatment took about five months and created a ghastly stench that my mother tried to overcome with liberal sprinklings of lavender water and other perfumes.

I visited my brother with Amah and we saw him with his leg strapped up in a sling, the exposed flesh lightly covered with gauze, playing a board game with one of the other patients. Gordon was never again allowed to play contact sports or walk or run too much. Instead he developed his athletic abilities by becoming a superb swimmer and water polo player.

Our freewheeling existence had to end. By May or June adults set up a school, that we attended for one hour each day. Classes were staggered as there were only two small rooms allocated in G-Block. The teachers were volunteers and not all were trained in teaching. The curriculum was basic English and Arithmetic, with some French and Latin for those nine years and over. The Japanese had agreed to the prisoners setting up a school on condition the children were not taught any History or Geography. They seemed to think these subjects would make us proud of our background, rebellious, and if we managed to escape, perhaps too knowledgeable on local geography.

Before this school was organized my mother and three neighbouring parents had formed a study group of four girls to take part in an hour of tutoring each day. The others were Doreen Hunt, a pretty, dark-haired girl, Isabel Gomersall, slim and fair-haired, and Anne, who was brown-haired and rather shorter than the rest of us, with a more stocky build.

We were from diverse backgrounds. Doreen's mother was American and her British father was in the police force. Isabel's father was a wealthy businessman and her mother a very fair Englishwoman. Anne's father was an accountant or lawyer with a business firm. Despite the differences in our backgrounds, we had been brought together by our parents' similar regard for having us well educated.

We had enough in common that we tended to play together as well as having other friends. When we first started our special study group we were annoyed with Isabel for constantly telling us what a large house she had lived in – and especially about a dining room seating twenty people. We felt she was boasting. And when Isabel reminisced we remembered with sadness our own, albeit smaller, homes. We asked her not to do it. Isabel seemed surprised, but stopped.

My mother supervised Spelling and Dictation with us, and Doreen's mother taught Arithmetic. An Anglican clergyman, the Reverend Hadwen, was a substitute for Anne's parents. He was an academically inclined, unworldly, pleasant, slim, fair man who wore rimless glasses. Despite the Japanese ban, the Reverend Hadwen taught us Geography, which in this case consisted of memorizing all the towns on the railway routes in southern England. He stood tentatively in front of a large map of England he put up on the wall of his cubicle and with a long ruler pointed out the towns. In addition he volunteered some information about Jersey cows, their appearance and excellent capacity at producing milk. After class the Reverend Hadwen took down the map and hid it under his bed.

We tended to misbehave in the Reverend Hadwen's class. Within a few months, Anne and (no doubt to his relief) the Reverend Hadwen, left our group.

Isabel's mother was a very retiring person, who always turned away when I went to their door to talk to Isabel. She did not teach us. Instead Isabel's father, a very intelligent, perceptive man with large, dark eyes, improved our general knowledge. In the warmer evenings we sat outside with Mr. Gomersall who told us informative stories. One evening he said his story was especially for me – about a Scottish engineer and bridge-builder called Charles Telford (similar to Telfer, my surname). During these occasions I thought sadly of classes with my own father before the Japanese secret police took him away.

After a month or two Mr. Hayashi considerably changed our living conditions. That was when we started to have cutbacks in our food and beatings for not following the rules. There was an almost total ban on outside hospital care for all prisoners, and on dental and eye care including the renewal of eyeglasses or the obtaining of new prescriptions. The Japanese were charging the Allies too much for these medical services and they refused to pay for them. We just accepted this state of affairs. No one seemed to think this was very heroic. It was the kind of adjustment all civilians involved in the war were making. But it did make us feel more forlorn, removed from the world we had known before.

The lack of eye care affected me, as it was soon after that the general school started. At the one hour of classes I attended, a trained primary school teacher was in charge. It was then that we both realized I could not see the board. At the Cathedral Girls' School, I'd been separately tutored sitting at a little table, and had not needed to look at a board. An optician among the prisoners found I was near-sighted. There was no question of having glasses prescribed, and from then on I was allowed to go up to the blackboard to read it.

At this early stage in my being short sighted I did not find it a disadvantage. Being myopic was all I knew.

15. New Activities

As well as those who taught us in school, there were other wonderful people in the camp, who took up the task of keeping children busy in a productive and entertaining way, providing many outlets other than school for our energy and interests. They also gave me some of the happiest and funniest experiences of my childhood in the camp.

The Reverend and Mrs. Hancock quickly set up a Sunday school that met in the concert hall in the T-Block end of the camp. My mother played the piano and Mr. and Mrs. Hancock gave lessons from bible readings. Mrs. Hancock also led the singing of hymns and of other religious songs familiar to us.

One Sunday my brother and his friends were more fidgety than usual. They whispered together, their arms about each other's shoulders, and burst into suppressed laughter. Mrs. Hancock offered us the usual free choice for the last hymn to sing. The boys all shouted out they would like to sing "Build on the Rock", and at last we found out what all the joking was about. It was some of the words mentioned, "the earthquake's shock." This part was accompanied by our feet crashing to the ground – an action my brother and his friends, of course, greatly enjoyed On this occasion when we came to "the earthquake's shock" they began to stamp their feet unnecessarily noisily on the wood floor, and also at other points in the song where it was inappropriate. The boys went wild banging on the floor. They found this so hilarious they couldn't stop laughing.

This caused poor Mrs. Hancock to break down and start berating the boys. Later, their parents scolded them. One of these (my mother) was on the spot, playing the piano for the tunes we sang. She went into immediate action and ordered Gordon to our room for the rest of the day.

As I was coming back from the T-Camp concert hall where we had Sunday school, I couldn't help thinking about the summers by the sea and the Sunday school we had there.

On Sundays at the seaside we children gathered together at the request of missionaries. They gave a session, which consisted mainly of singing, to which we all looked forward.

"Jesus bids us shine with a pure, clear light," we sang as we sat on the beach, in our summer clothes and floppy cotton hats. And, "I am the resurrection and the life."

At the beach Gordon told me stories of wonderful gardens farther out beneath the sea, with brightly coloured sea plants and fish. We swam out and he tried to take me down to see the gardens. Several times we dived; Gordon held my hand to give me greater speed, but each time I struggled free and we resurfaced. I didn't have the lung capacity to stay under long enough to make the trip. Imagined gardens, drawn from my brother's descriptions, were all that I possessed at the end.

And so the soft summer days slid slowly away to the mesmerizing murmur of the sea. As we played in the sand

and found rock pools with their enchanting, miniature sea-gardens, idyllic sunlit days on the beach stretched seemingly endlessly to the remote time when summer would be over.

During the week at Yu Yuen Road there was dancing. We learned a little tap and modern dance but the major influence in our dancing lives was Mrs. Edwards, who taught us ballet in-depth. She was a "white" (i.e. anti-Communist) Russian married to a British man, still danced well herself and had played in, and also choreographed for several silent movies. We regarded her as a rather exotic person, to be respected. She taught in a very professional manner.

In the concert hall at T-Block, she put us through our paces with a "Von, Two, Tree …" We had no *barre* equipment. On good weather days we practised our back bends on the grass behind G-Block. I was never able to do a back bend. One day Mrs. Edwards watched me as I tried and said, "If I could have you when you are tree, *then* I could do somethink with you!"

Despite my lack of suppleness Mrs. Edwards regarded me as reliable. She chose me to lead the *corps de ballet* onto the stage at the right moment in the course of concerts. During our time at Yu Yuen Road we put on two or three ballet shows and worked very hard practising for them.

We performed a similar number of modern dance shows, one of which was for Easter. I was a (relatively) large rabbit standing beside a big Easter egg made of two large baskets covered with brown paper. When I whispered through the paper that it was the right time, some small rabbits (three or four years old) were to burst through and do a dance. We were just about to open the stage curtains when one little rabbit said, "I want to go to the bathroom." This feeling was infectious. Soon there was a chorus of, "I want to go to the bathroom." The harried mothers had to unpick and re-sew almost all of the costumes before we could open the show for an increasingly restive audience.

Life was not all singing and dancing. We were supposed to help in running the camp. The prisoners' administration committee decided the men would do the rough work in the camp sick bay and the mass cooking required. My mother played the piano for all camp concerts and the Sunday school. She also helped on the camp's welfare committee. (This committee helped persuade the prisoners not to annoy the Japanese guards. The internees well knew about the atrocities against the Chinese, and feared that as the war progressed to the disadvantage of Japan, it could lead to reprisals against us, in particular if we gave the guards any trouble.) My brother became one of the official cobblers and spent increasing amounts of his time mending shoes as they wore out.

The very young (children under ten) did not have formal camp-running work but my mother said I had to set the table for family meals and grind the maize we were given to make bread during the first few months of our confinement. This was where my previous wanderings in the country were useful, as we ground the flour using a stone quern, which stood in an archway between the back and front of G-Block. It was very familiar to me, being exactly like those Michael West and I saw in the farms outside the Seventh Day Adventist village. Instead of a donkey or a cow to push the handle to turn the stone block, there was me.

It was hard work for a seven year old but we regarded

these tasks as fun, and helped each other. I never had to grind our maize all by myself. The responsibilities we took drove us forward into greater maturity. We felt proud about taking charge of duties that affected not only us but our families as well. Gordon was treated as an adult, doing work for the good of the camp as a whole.

Many friends were in the same camp as us and we saw them working hard at jobs that were very menial in relation to what they were accustomed to before. Work in the kitchen was particularly gruelling as it involved heavy lifting in high temperatures. Men did this work, although a woman would guide them at first on how to cook. Mr. Robertson gave the cooks a severe lecture about pilfering food. He said everyone must have his fair share of what was available, if we were all to survive. The scrapings from the rice vat were to be carefully put aside and given to children who were growing. He further said he'd be making unannounced visits himself and if he found any irregularities, he'd remove the culprit and publicize his name.

Our mothers used the communal kitchens to bake with the flour. This was how things were in the beginning when we received maize to supplement our food. But within a few months, the situation changed, and we no longer received our maize allowance. We had to rely on irregular donations of weevilly porridge from the Red Cross.

By the time my first birthday in the camp came along in April, food had already become noticeably scarce, and I assumed my mother would not be able to do much if anything to mark the day. I began to daydream about parties at Bubbling Well Road and at friends' houses.

My birthday party was always the same, quite small and very British – or at least European. Three other girls came for tea when we had sandwiches and cake. The cake was always the same: a chocolate cake with curls of marzipan around the edges on the top. The cake was always delivered from Kiesling and Bader.

Mine was by no means the typical children's birthday party given by British parents in Shanghai. They were normally much larger affairs, which often featured a show of Laurel and Hardy and Charlie Chaplin films from Hollywood, a magician or Chinese acrobats dressed in colourful clothes.

On my first birthday in camp, when I was seven, my mother made a red jelly. She put it on the window-ledge overnight to set in the cool of the darker hours.

In the afternoon she ran in: *disaster.*

"I forgot about your jelly," she said.

We brought in the jelly. It had melted in the sun.

"Well, we'll just drink the jelly," said my mother. And to celebrate my birthday, that is what we ceremoniously did. We divided the red liquid equally into each of our three tin mugs, and then *drank* it, laughing. My mother then gave me a big birthday hug, and Gordon gave his version: a light boxing tap on my arm.

There were activities for the young adults as well. Mrs. Edwards arranged for them to put on a play *Neptune's Kingdom* with mosquito nets and lamps covered in green paper producing an impression of water.

Some other single younger people made their own amusement. Every Saturday evening Vera, Dudley and

George met for dinner in their cleanest, best clothes. They set up a table with wildflowers in a jar and a candle, and added some of their store of canned food to that evening's dinner. For several hours the three reminisced about travel, books they'd read and plays seen or concerts attended.

One Saturday, Vera brought some records to play on George's gramophone. There were a variety of songs by the distinguished American baritone Nelson Eddy, some sung in Russian.

"Listen to this record. Before he became a film star, Nelson Eddy was lead baritone with the Philadelphia Grand Opera, supposed to go on to the Metropolitan Opera in New York. Mrs. Edwards says Eddy's accent in Russian is so good he could have been brought up in a Russian-speaking household. By the way, she tells me her first name is Tamara."

And so they listened to the beautiful, perfectly trained voice of Nelson Eddy singing Prince Gremin's tender aria from Tchaikovsky's opera *Eugene Onegin* in praise of his adorable young wife Tatyana, and then heard other records. The three friends reminisced about films they'd seen featuring Nelson Eddy and Jeanette MacDonald : their first, *Naughty Marietta* set in France and the New World, and most recently *Bitter Sweet*. Vera had kept some of the programs the Shanghai movie theatres produced, outlining in Chinese and English the plot of the film being shown.

They agreed that *Sweethearts*, mainly played in modern dress without the period costumes of the other films, probably showed the two stars most like what they were in real life. Vera, George and Dudley wondered what films Jeanette MacDonald and Nelson Eddy were making now.

They would also be entertaining American troops. The previous world seemed so remote. The three young people felt so cut off, marking time until they could resume their lives.

The man designated to listen to the illegal radio strained to hear the distant sound from the American west coast station KGEI. Allied forces had blockaded sea access to Japan. The Japanese were effectively cut off from supplies coming to them across the Co-Prosperity Sphere. The tide of war was turning in favour of the Allies.

16. Nature and Human Nature

Our move to the Seventh Day Adventists' village had brought me more into contact with Nature than before. Strangely, our confinement in the first internment camp continued to bring this natural world more to my attention.

I was sitting aimlessly, drawing the face of an elf on the concrete playground in front of G-Block with school chalk when a friend came and said, "Come quickly and see!" We ran to the playing field and in the middle was a magical sight: a swarm of hundreds of dragonflies. The iridescent colours of their transparent wings sparkled in the sun as they wheeled about. Enchanted, and without thinking, I walked forward until I was in the middle of the shimmering mass of insects. I imagined myself up in the sky in the middle of a rainbow – until the dragonflies soared away and I returned to real life.

Uncle Steve Wilkinson had brought several hives of bees into the camp to provide honey as extra food. He put the hives on the edge of T-Camp. Uncle Steve explained the life cycle of the bee to my brother and me and showed us the marvellous structure inside the hive where the honey-making sections were. Most prisoners had never before seen bees *en masse*, and one day some curious people took the lids off the hives and forgot to put them back. A rainstorm at night killed all the bees.

While at the camp Gordon also pursued his interest in Nature. He was able to add to his collection of winged insects (dead and mounted on boards) when he captured a magnificent Moon Moth in the camp. I marvelled at the moth. It was three or four inches across and had beautiful, greenish-white wings with a rounded white marking on each wing in the shape of the moon.

In the summer afternoons we children often gathered under a large willow tree near T-Camp and talked. (The trunk of the tree ran almost parallel to the ground before curving upright.) On one occasion I saw on the bark of the willow a beautiful, whole skin of an insect, something like a two-inch long fly, complete with perfect, transparent wings folded along the back. My brother said it was the skin of a cicada, or "scissor grinder" as we called them because of the metallic sound they made in the tops of the trees when the weather was very hot. The sound rose to a crescendo before dying away – and then starting all over again.

Some found the camp experience frayed their nerves and brought out an annoyance with minor matters. Sometimes a mother whose child had not been chosen for an entertainment we were rehearsing arrived in a fury and announced there was some favouritism in the selection process. This was probably true with respect to me, as I suspect I was pushed into these because my mother was playing the piano, my brother was singing, and I would have been left alone during practices.

Before we went into the internment camp I was aware that adults regarded racial differences as being important. I knew the people outside our compound were racially different from us, and that some of the people we knew did not regard mixed marriages favourably. The children of these marriages were called "Eurasians." I had seen the Japanese ill treatment of the Chinese because they thought them inferior. However, in spite of all this background information I had not yet come into personal contact with racism.

This first experience happened in Yu Yuen Road where there were two Jewish families: the Benjamins and the Abrahams. They were of British nationality and so lived in the camp with us. Although they kept strictly to themselves, we could not help being aware of these people, closely packed as we were.

The Benjamins were a young family, very beautiful, something special. They were not very tall. Mrs. Benjamin dressed in long clothes coming down to the ground. She moved gracefully around with her three children usually close beside her.

One hot afternoon three members of our study group were talking together under the trees behind G-Block. The cicadas were sporadically grinding their sound up above. Esther, the eldest Benjamin child, came and asked to play. It was a brief visit.

Esther was about a year younger than we were. Her skin glowed and her dark brown eyes and curly hair sparkled. She was a shining child. Anne quickly took over the conversation. She asked Esther if she had washed yet that day, and whether she had cleaned the maggots from between her toes. I took these comments literally and looked at Esther's clean appearance and clean bare feet. As Esther sadly turned to go away without answering, the cicadas' metallic grinding rose to a deafening crescendo. Doreen and I were taken by surprise and didn't have the presence of mind to react until after Esther has gone. We asked Anne why she would say such things to Esther but she didn't reply.

Later that day I told my mother what had happened and asked what it was about. My mother told me the Benjamins were Jewish, and that the German government was persecuting Jewish people in Europe. Even in Shanghai some people were against the Jewish people. She said this was no more acceptable than the way the Japanese hated the Chinese. After that time Anne did not come to our study group. I thought it had something to do with her behaviour towards Esther.

The Abrahams were a larger, older family than the Benjamins. Their father, with his long beard, seemed ancient; the mother seemed middle-aged. The six children ranged in age from young adults in their late teens to a two year old baby. My brother became friends with Abraham (Abe) Abraham, a boy of about seventeen. Abe knew how to mend shoes and taught my brother the craft.

After the shoe leather Abe had brought to the camp ran out, they made soles for shoes out of leather suitcases people gave them.

The Abrahams were from an order of Jewish people who would not do anything to create light after sundown on Fridays. They asked my brother to come and switch on the light for them on that day of the week. So once a week from then on Gordon would feel his way in the blackout, down the scary, dark passage to the Abrahams' room, where the family were sitting with the curtains drawn, and turn on the five-watt bulb for the father to start their religious observances by reading from the Torah.

My brother paused in an evening stroll and saw one of the sick bay workers being challenged by a guard. As part of his camp duties in protecting our health the prisoner was squatting down picking up a large mound of catarrhal sputum left by a coolie delivering our next day's food. He held up the rag he was using and the guard turned away with a disgusted grunt. As the fellow captive stood up my brother could see that he was shaking with fear.

"What's wrong?"

"Best you don't know what just almost happened."

Later the sick bay worker unfolded the message on fine silk he'd taken from some thin rubber film contained in the spittle. It said two internee radio operators in Pootung camp had been found out and tortured in Bridge House before being sent to Haiphong Road, the *Kempeitai's* jail where my father was.

17. Looking for a Father

I rushed into our room, slamming the outer and inner doors, and threw myself on my bed, sobbing. Mrs. Sanbrook called through the wall to ask what was the matter. I didn't reply but, in between my crying, started to sing, over and over again a song, which was about me and my true love meeting again, on the bonny banks of Loch Lomond.

It was a song my father taught me when I was three. I wondered *when* we would ever meet again.

Later my mother returned from one of her camp chores, helping with the sick bay patients. I heard her talking quietly to Mrs. Sanbrook. Then my mother came in and sat me beside her on her bed. She put her arm around me and reminisced about my father and how much he enjoyed playing croquet and ball games with me, and reading and talking to me. Discussing these times seemed to bring them back. My mother said Daddy had not forgotten us, and assured me that we would see him again when the war was over. For a while, she seemed to forget me and looked into the distance. I knew she was remembering her own times with my father.

We once had a half-hour visit to Haiphong Road where

families congregated in a large hall, clustering round their father who, by order of the Japanese, sat on a chair. There was news from my father every month, in a 25-word letter printed in capitals on a form. After a few months, letters came, but all the words were blocked out with thick black ink: censored. On the first camp Christmas, and the second, we received a hand-drawn Christmas card. The 1944 card had a Christmas tree outside and a self-portrait of my father inside. He drew the other fathers (in his camp) whose families were also in ours and in other camps around Shanghai. From his sketch we could see that my father looked strained as well as thinner and older than before.

In a way I had substitute fathers at this time. I had regular contact with Mr. Gomersall. During his talks with our study group he provided a calm and wise presence. However, the most unusual father for me was a Chinese policeman I met while playing in the field behind B-Block.

Adjacent to one corner of the camp, at the other end of B-Block from our room, was the station of the Shanghai Municipal Fire Brigade, manned by Chinese. On top of the fire station was a tall tower from which Japanese guards surveyed the camp. An empty garage of the fire station backed on the camp's grounds and beside it was a gate in the high fence around the camp. Here a Chinese policeman always stood. At first I didn't notice him as, on my mother's instructions, I never went near the fence.

One day I was playing with a ball in the field behind B-Block when it bounced away. I ran after the ball, looked up after picking it up, and there suddenly, just in front of me, was a Chinese policeman in uniform. I didn't remember seeing him before. I went over to talk, and said my father was also a policeman and that I missed him very much. I told him my father's name and the policeman said he knew him, and that he was a very good man.

After the first encounter I went to talk to the Chinese policeman quite regularly. He asked me what I was doing just now, apart from the times I was playing in the field and he could see me. I told him about my friends and the concerts and my reading and school. He took a real interest in how I was progressing and cheered me on.

Once when I went to see my new friend he was not at his usual post by the gate. I found him in the fire station garage torturing a bird by sticking a pin into it. I asked him to let it go, and the bird managed to flutter away. I thought sadly of my real father trying to revive my dying pet canary with an eyedropper full of brandy.

I am sitting comfortably in my parents' bed, propped up and surrounded by mounds of feather pillows. In front of me is the large white folding bed table we use for having meals in bed when we are ill. I am recovering from measles. Although my care is almost totally in the hands of Amah, my mother always looks after us when we are unwell. My mother and Amah are fussing over me, as I will not eat anything. They put all sorts of tempting vegetables, fruit and jellies before me but I'm not interested.

Then Amah comes in with a plate of potatoes mashed with carrots. As she carefully places the dish before me, her expression is one of cautious hope. I find the mix of colours interesting and decide to try this new dish. It tastes good, and at last I am eating. Ah Ling's expression changes to one of intense relief. I can see Amah and my mother are very pleased.

I woke up from this dream, in our room at Yu Yuen Road, ill with jaundice. There was no wide bed, no soft pillows, and much worse, no Amah. This time I stayed in bed for two or three weeks, unable to eat the cooked camp food because of the extreme nausea the smell of it caused me. My mother was given some bread with margarine, and I ate that until I recovered. The camp doctor had no medicines, but he brought a clove of garlic. I had a little of it but didn't like the taste, so my brother ate it.

When I was up again I went to see the policeman, and he asked why I hadn't come for so long. The policeman was sorry to hear I had been ill, and the next time I saw him, he gave me a beautiful head of a Chinese goddess, about two inches high, which he had carved himself. It was made of terra cotta. He said it would protect me from further sickness and I should keep it. Our room had two small windows and between them was a loose brick. I put the goddess's head away in the secret hiding place behind the loose brick, and was not ill again from jaundice while we were at Yu Yuen Road.

18. Winter

Food, or rather the lack of it, was an important part of our camp experience. On the first evening as prisoners we lined up in the Boys' School assembly hall and were startled to be presented with strips of raw fish and rice. These were laid out on trays placed on tables, like a buffet meal: Sushi, I suppose. After some discussion with Mr. Kawasaki this food was replaced with European cuisine. Fairly quickly after his successor took charge this gave way to the rather Spartan diet to which we became accustomed.

Breakfast was "congee", a paste of rice and water, which became increasingly thin over time. We fended for ourselves for lunch; this consisted at first of bread, peanut butter and "mesuami" (pronounced: mee-zyu-ah-mee) a syrupy substance that with the bread and peanut butter tasted fine to us children. The peanut butter and mesuami came from parcels occasionally sent to the camp by the Red Cross. For dinner we again lined up with our enamelled tin bowls to receive a ladle-full of soup. As time went by this soup became increasingly thin. I overheard one of the men who did the cooking saying they were given two pounds of some unidentified meat to feed over three hundred people in B-Block. (There were about a thousand prisoners in Yu Yuen Road camp.)

I wondered what kind of meat the soup contained; and thought of the first pet I could remember. He was a large white rabbit called Peter, who lived in a roomy hutch on the veranda. During the day Peter hopped about the house, being treated like a dog or cat. He followed Lesley McLaren and me around as we went up or down stairs, or out into the garden.

One night my mother thought she heard the garden gate creak. She went out on the balcony but couldn't see anything. In the morning we found Peter had gone. Someone had stolen him, possibly for food, which had become scarce in Shanghai by that time. I hoped our soup was not made from someone's pet rabbit. This thought made me dislike meat even more than before.

The grey, watery soup usually had a little cabbage floating in it. We considered ourselves lucky to receive part of a cabbage leaf with our soup. Sometimes when we were playing behind B-Block after breakfast, the cooks called us into the kitchens and gave us pieces of crisp, burned rice that they had scraped off the sides of the huge urns of congee. Delicious!

Occasionally we received Red Cross parcels containing boiled, coloured candies (or sweets as we called them), some jellies and powdered eggs, or porridge. This food was shared out equally. The one time I helped carry my family's share it was a small bowl of the boiled sweets of many colours. I thought they looked too wonderful actually to eat.

Very quickly then, our diet became one of watery rice, watery soup, some bread and sometimes a little peanut butter and syrup. Strangely I do not remember once wishing for the food we had previously. Perhaps this had something to do with the fact that so far I had always been a finicky eater, not interested in food. I had always refused to eat meat and its absence did not bother me. Unlike the others, who complained, I accepted the new circumstances with respect to food. However, like everyone else I often felt very hungry.

In spite of the increasing troubles, during the first Christmas in camp we had a wonderful time. On that first Christmas we still had the materials we had brought with us to make presents. One cold November morning I was sitting on my bed embroidering a green and red Christmas motif on a handkerchief for my mother. Aunt Ivy had given me the threads, needles, a handkerchief and some sewing lessons. I had drawn some holly and berries on the cloth with a pencil. And now all I had to do was fill it in.

I sat undoing knots that had magically appeared in the threads – when along came my brother.

"Ha, ha, making a mess of it," he teased. "You can't sew," (too true). "I could do it better myself," he jeered, turning to look out the window.

My temper boiled *up*. I ran and jabbed my needle into the posterior of that hateful boy. "Yah *aahh*!" yelled Gordon, rubbing the painful spot and turning round. At first he gave a brief laugh when he saw me standing, the needle pointed forward like a tiny lance.

Then he returned to his usual pedantic self.

"You should be more careful what you do. The needle

could have broken off in me," he said. "There might be germs on it."

I looked anxiously at the needle and thought, *Thank goodness; it's not broken – and it looks clean.*

As I was busy making a present for my mother, she was also busy – making a present for me. Parents went secretively to each other's rooms to make surprise gifts. For several nights before the Christmas of 1943 Mrs. Duncan came to our room to make a carryall bag for Sheila. The bag, with handles, was made of thick red cotton with a lively yellow pattern and lined in yellow. Mrs. Duncan sewed a miniature version for me. Some evenings, my mother went off to the Duncans' room.

There was concern in the camp for little Jose Chamberlain. In the Autumn her mother had died and the Japanese would not release her father from Haiphong Road to look after her. Several women had offered to move in with her temporarily or at least to share with her at night. But Jose had chosen to stay as she was: as her father's friends, the McFarlanes, were through the cubicle wall to refer to if she needed anything at night. During the day she went to the Toons, another couple who were friends of her family, who agreed to be her guardians until the war ended and her father could take over. The Toons had no camp duties as they were elderly.

But soon Jose faced another loss when Mr. Toon died. Jose and Mrs. Toon agreed to move into a hut in T-Camp together and that was the arrangement until her father returned after the war. Jose was an independent child, with real character, and highly intelligent. I knew, because she was in a school class with me.

During that holiday my tendency to be religious was reinforced by what I regarded as proof of the power of prayer. For months before the event I prayed for some paper dolls (printed, not hand-made) with paper clothes to change their outfits. In early December we received a parcel sent by my father's former secretary with whom he had left money. The parcel had food in it and we had to open it immediately. When I unwrapped my present I was overjoyed to see paper dolls.

The dolls were not quite what I had wanted, as they represented Christopher Robin and his toy friends. But God works in mysterious ways. They were undeniably paper dolls with sets of clothes for Christopher Robin – and a true miracle in my eyes. Gordon's gift was an adventure book and there was perfume for my mother. We enjoyed the bacon and chocolates that came as well. My mother rationed out the chocolates, but we had the bacon right away with our congee at breakfast until it was finished. That took a few days.

All the families whose fathers were in Haiphong Road received a Christmas card drawn by my father with the design by another internee: J.A.E.S.B. (Joseph Albert E. Sanders Bates.) The sketches showed a no doubt rather idealised set of activities in the camp and had printed on it an inspiring verse by W.E.Henley.

Before the actual date, we prisoners put on a Christmas show in the hall at T-camp. The Japanese had been invited, and after we were all seated the camp commandant and a few of his most senior guards marched stiffly in to some seats we had reserved at the front.

The show's opening scene was of the three Magi

sweeping across the stage singing "We three kings from Orient are." My brother (one of the kings) was resplendent in a bright blue silk dressing gown of our mother's. The surplus skirt trailed magnificently behind as he walked. His height was enhanced by a kingly white turban, which was made from a bath towel.

Held high on the end of a stick by a small child in the wings, the outline head of a camel poked out behind the Magi. It wobbled dangerously as the child struggled to keep it in view of the audience. To the uncritical spectators, the camel appeared to nod cheerily to everyone. We all joined in singing carols. The Christmas show was a tremendous success, and even the Japanese, looking rather puzzled by it all, clapped politely.

On Christmas morning, Gordon woke us up as usual before dawn and we looked for our presents, which my mother had left on our beds. There were no pillowcases bulging with toys. There was no being sent back to bed by my mother with the gift we liked best – as there was exactly one for each of us from our mother. Gordon's present was a knitted scarf in bright red. Mine was a bed for the teddy bear and doll. It was made from a large cardboard box, with a bed head of cardboard, all covered in light green satiny material. The bed had some sheets and a pink coverlet. I thought it was beautiful. I gave our mother the handkerchief I'd embroidered with holly, and she said she'd use it every Christmas day from then on. Then my mother brought out another gift – for me, from Mrs. Duncan. It was the wonderful, colourful bag. I ran along the corridor to thank her, and Mrs. Duncan gave me a big hug.

From then on, I used the bag for my books, and took it

to school; at night the bear and the doll, the king and queen of my domain, went to sleep in the bed my mother made. Their pet the blue giraffe slept with me. I hugged his soft stuffed body, and his long neck stretched out to allow his cheerful, friendly head to face mine.

19. Reading

My toys were my stable companions. When I had a book to read, I sat on the bed beside them. That winter I wrapped myself in my blanket for warmth. The bear, the doll, the blue giraffe and I sat on the bed and I read all my books over and over again. Also I was able to borrow some, which had been left behind in the school. These contained improving sorts of stories written for Victorian children. Their religious themes further strengthened my own belief.

In particular, *Christie's Old Organ* by Mrs. O.F. Walton made a great impression on me. I read it many times. The book was about an orphan named Christie who slept in the doorway of a house until he was taken in by an old man (Treffy), who occupied a bare room and made his living by playing an old barrel organ in the streets. People threw a copper into the old man's hat if they liked the music or felt sorry for him.

The old man, and later the boy Christie, turned a handle in the side of the organ and it played tunes. The tunes were out of date and the organ was badly worn. It stood between two large wheels and had long, wheelbarrow-like handles attached to it. The sides were decorated with sunlit scenes of Italy, quite unlike the cold, drab streets where the organ played. Christie and Treffy didn't make much money.

When the old man died Christie continued with the organ. One picture in the book shows a warmly dressed little girl bringing food in a basket to a ragged Christie. Christie joined a religious organization, which educated him. He became a helper in a country parish, married a young woman who was also a member of the religious group, and lived happily ever after.

In the closing paragraph of *Christie's Old Organ* Christie wrote to his benefactor that now he could think of Christie and his wife living happily in an Earthly home while still anticipating with pleasure their Heavenly one.

The tone of the story and the assured happy ending comforted me. I felt I was almost in the same situation as Christie: lacking one parent, feeling very cold and hungry, and living in a bare room. I hoped that surely things would turn out for the best for me also.

It was during these solitary reading sessions, as I sat with my toys around me, that I came fully to realize our circumstances were not all fun and social life. They really had changed. I longed for the comfortable armchairs we had left behind. I had taken them so much for granted, and yet now they seemed the utmost in luxury. They came to epitomize the secure and comfortable life I had lost. I thought about all the books my father had read to me, and the music we played on our gramophone, that we had to wind up at the side to make it start.

At one of the occasions when I was reading and remembering, two or three weeks after Christmas, my mother came and told me Mrs. Duncan had a pain in her chest and my mother would be going to sit with her.

I felt crushed. I was not accustomed to people I knew suffering. Previously if anyone was ill we would call Doctor Burton and he could always do something to help. Now, there was little our camp doctor could do. He had no painkillers, not even an aspirin.

On this occasion, to escape from the camp's reality, I started to daydream about times in Bubbling Well Road; I lifted the blue giraffe off the bed and gave him a hug ...

The snake lies neatly coiled on a tread of the flight of stairs, his head in position, cleanly sliced off. I wonder how such a soft-slithery-wild thing has come into this hard place of stone and marble, and have a fleeting vision of the snake in a garden with grass and bushes. I think that perhaps he came in to be cooler – a fatal mistake. The "boy" is putting away his knife, and after a short conversation with Amah, resumes cleaning the window of the landing for the apartment stairs we are climbing.

As I follow Amah and Gordon I tense at the thought of the new, and to us famous, person we are about to meet.

What will I *say* to her? I wail to myself.

My brother and I, with Amah, have come to see "Aunt Peggy" who lives in a flat or apartment near our compound on Bubbling Well Road, a residential area in Shanghai's International Settlement in China. She will present me with a prize I have won, for colouring, in a contest held by Shanghai's local radio station's Children's Hour.

Aunt Peggy was always running competitions: story and song-writing competitions, painting and drawing competitions and – at last – a colouring competition, of a train, for money. I, at four years old, had been demanding pocket money for some months but with no result. In our family, a regular allowance was only for those six years or older.

The colouring competition (for children under eight years old) was my big opportunity to have money of my own and the freedom to spend it on whatever I chose. I imagined myself going to the huge Wing On's department store on Nanking Road. I would grandly put down my $3.00 (Shanghai) prize, which I assumed would buy what I wanted: some pencils and a note book to write in, for my own private extra use when I started school and learned to write.

My brother Gordon was eight years old, and was always drawing and making things – or taking things apart and putting them together again. It made sense to ask his advice about the train colouring competition.

"Keep the colours inside the lines of the drawing," he said. "Don't go over the lines."

I lay on the rug in front of the fireplace with the drawing and some crayons. Working very carefully I started to crayon the train red and green with black wheels. The railway track was grey, with brown trestles. The sky was blue (no clouds). Gordon came in and frowned as he saw the messy colouring starting to emerge, and without thinking he tidied the edges with an eraser and finished the picture. As a last touch, he added some black smoke, curling out of the stack and streaming back over the train as he imagined it rushing along.

The picture had won the competition and this was how my Amah, Gordon and I were climbing the stairs (as the elevator was out of order) to the fourth floor of Aunt Peggy's building.

We ring the bell and Aunt Peggy ushers us in to a large living room, and we all stand around on a thick woolen rug in front of the unlit electric fireplace. I am at just below the height of her waist, gazing up at this person who is familiar through her radio program but whom I have never before seen. Aunt Peggy seems very tall with long legs encased in sheer silk stockings and feet clad in high-heeled shoes. As I look way up I see her hair is long, shining and light brown; she is beautiful. My brother is enchanted. As usual I am nervous in the company of a new person, especially someone as famous as Aunt Peggy.

Like me, Aunt Peggy doesn't seem particularly at ease. She does not talk to us or offer any hospitality but quickly brings up the subject of the contest. I stand on the woolly rug in front of the fireplace to receive my prize, wondering what to say. In a haze of disappointment I hear Aunt Peggy's voice:

"We thought you would be older. As you are so young, I have bought you a toy."

A toy! I think in horror, what about the *money*?

Seeing my expression she quickly adds, "It cost a *lot* more than $3.00."

Turning from a chair with something in her hands, she presents me with the prize – a large blue stuffed animal. The royal blue giraffe stands almost two feet tall. It has a red felt mane down its long neck and a red felt saddle across its back. There is a short red felt tail, cut into a tassel at the end, and floppy blue, redlined ears. The bright glass eyes twinkle in a friendly way, and the mouth turns up in a smile.

The toy is really a cross between a giraffe and a horse – and for me it is love at first sight. Somehow the short interview ends, and we say "Goodbye." I hug the soft blue body of the giraffe and his head flops over my shoulder.

On the way home the noisy, colourful pageant of Bubbling Well Road passed me by. I walked along between Amah and Gordon and scarcely heard their conversation – or saw the surroundings.

By now, our first winter as prisoners, the blue giraffe was becoming a little worn by my hugs, a little dirty from sitting on the floor beside my other toys. I remembered how bright his colours had been when I first saw him; the red mane and tail still shone out, but the blue was fading. I decided he needed some extra care. So I put him on my bed during the day as well as at night.

20. Getting Serious

In the "Pure Brightness" (Ching-ming) of early April, my second birthday in camp came along. As usual the one-more-bottle bird announced the coming of spring; it was our equivalent of the cuckoo and seemed to sing "one more bottle". In the days when I was being urged to drink it, my mother told me the bird was asking for one more bottle of milk. I was eight years old, and there was no question of a present or anything nice to eat. Gordon followed our father's example by scrounging a piece of paper and drawing me a birthday card, with flowers on it and A Happy Birthday inside. We put the card on our table by the window. My mother gave me a hug and I really did feel happy.

The big surprise was from Aunt Ivy, who came to our room after breakfast and the presentation of my birthday card. Behind her back she had a parcel, wrapped in birthday wrapping paper! I was so excited as I carefully opened it. There inside was another baby doll; but this time it had black skin and a straw hula skirt. Aunt Ivy said she'd brought it to keep for me when I didn't have any birthday present. The new doll was beautiful – and there was just enough space for her in the doll's bed beside the teddy bear and my other doll. I thought this birthday was the best I'd ever seen.

It was about this time that Isabel, Doreen and I hatched a scheme for livening up our lives. We had read a book about girl detectives, and our idea was to hide under the bed in each of our rooms and observe and write down anything we saw or heard. The first room we tried was Doreen's. We all crawled in under her parents' bed and Isabel got a splinter in her knee from the wood floor. That almost stopped everything, but she decided to wait to have it taken out. The first half hour was extremely boring as no one came into the room, and we were almost giving up a second time when suddenly the door opened and in came Mr. Hunt.

He wandered about, preparing for some camp task he had to perform by putting on a pair of overalls. At least that's what we guessed he was doing, as all we could see were his feet and ankles. We had a school exercise book with us to take notes of any conversations; but being alone, he didn't say anything, neither did he sing or hum. My religious feelings began to surge up and I whispered to the others that we should come out from under the bed and let him know we were there – to be met by horrified sign language to the contrary from the others.

After Mr. Hunt had left the room we crawled out and agreed it wasn't as good an idea as we had thought. Then Mrs. Hunt entered and saw us all there, so we decided to tell her what we had done. At first she seemed concerned, but when we explained all that had happened, she relaxed and said we'd come to the right decision, not to do a repeat performance and to stop worrying about it. Mrs. Hunt gave us all a hug, and relieved, we went off to play outside.

During our second summer (1944) in Yu Yuen Road, in the wonderful warm and humid Shanghai weather that I so loved, we children had gathered together by the willow tree and it was then that we heard Mrs. (Nan) Duncan was returned to the camp from the hospital in a rickshaw, immediately after an operation for what had turned out to be her breast cancer, before she had regained consciousness. Some prisoners who happened to be walking past the guardhouse at a camp gate had seen Mrs. Duncan lying unconscious in the road where she had fallen when a coolie put down the shafts of the rickshaw bringing her from hospital. She appeared to have been lying there for some time in the heat, and they asked permission to bring her in, and took her to the camp's sickbay.

I thought of the kind attention Gordon received while he was at the Country Hospital. He had returned home in an ambulance. But we could see that now the situation was different. Poor Mrs. Duncan had not been so fortunate. She was in pain and there was nothing the camp doctor could give her to help. But after the surgical wounds healed, Mrs. Duncan seemed much better. We were all hoping for the war to end.

As the designated man listened to the news from Australia he shook his head. Saipan in the Marianas had fallen to U.S. troops in July 1944. General Saito and 31 thousand Japanese troops fought literally to the death in a twenty-three-day battle, which cost over three thousand American lives. Many Japanese civilians, urged on by the military, threw their children and themselves off cliffs at the island's northern tip. What would our local Japanese captors do before the end came? The prisoner wondered, *Would they murder all of us?*

Later, he drew on a cigarette (made of a mixture of rough Chinese tobacco and tea leaves) and said to his friend, with some irony, "Well the Allies have almost won the war, been saying that for over a year."

"What'll you do after the war's over?"

"Marry if my girl will have me, go to a country that's decent and stable, like Canada; have to re-qualify in the law."

"It's the terrible monotony, and the waiting, not knowing when our prison sentence will be over, wasting our lives."

We had begun to grow out of our clothes and shoes so the mothers set up what they called a barter mart where these items could be exchanged. Isabel, Doreen and I decided to help by finding other children with whom we could exchange clothes. Isabel's room was on the floor above Doreen's and mine. She had the clothes from her older sister and found a younger child on their floor of B-Block to whom she could hand on the ones she'd outgrown. Being one of the younger children, I did not fare too badly at first. I played with two sisters, who lived on the same floor of B-Block as us, and was proud to work out that I could give my clothes to the younger girl, and myself receive the older girl's outgrown garments. We had some trouble finding anyone to hand on garments to Doreen, who gave hers to her little sister, Lynn. So Doreen had to rely on the barter mart.

In summer the boys went barefoot to save on shoes. The soles of their feet became like wrinkled leather. The teenagers were the worst off. They had to dress in hand-me-downs from the adults. Despite our efforts, by the end of the war we became really ragged.

There was a particular problem providing warm clothing for the children who were changing in size. The winters in Shanghai can be very cold. We often had snow, and had no central heating in our rooms. In the better weather my mother and Aunt Ivy (Uncle Bill was in Haiphong Road with my father) sat out in deck chairs during the afternoons and evenings, unravelling old sweaters and knitting new ones.

The choice to bring deck chairs into the camp seemed idiosyncratic and an interesting reflection of the outlook on life our mothers had. In thinking about their imprisonment did they see themselves as having a lot of leisure – enough to spend some of it sitting in the sun in deck chairs? And why did they think this way? But the deck chairs proved to be very practical. They were the only ones we were able to bring into camp, no doubt because they folded up; and allowed our parents to have some sunshine while working. This practical aspect was probably one that my mother and Aunt Ivy had considered together as they prepared for camp life.

Food became even more scarce, and to keep from feeling too hungry, I drank a lot of water. When my mother and Aunt Ivy weren't there, Doreen and I sat on the two deck chairs talking. We swung back and forth on the canvas seats and often we could hear the water in my stomach sloshing around, which made Doreen and me laugh.

Always on the lookout for wool to knit clothes for my doll and teddy bear, I gathered the odd pieces my mother and Aunt Ivy cut off and threw away, tied them all together and amassed a huge ball, about five inches across, of multicoloured knitting wool. This ball of wool caused great envy and interest among the other girls and one of them offered to give me more wool than I had gathered if I would give her the ball of many colours. I accepted the offer and this led to my having even more wool to knit with, in a deep raspberry colour.

I invented an attractive new type of pattern, which my mother's friends asked me to teach them, so they could knit pretty sweaters for their daughters. The pattern managed to look lacy and bobbly at the same time. One friend of my mother's even used it for a baby's jacket.

Very few babies were born in camp, but one such birth ended tragically. The mother was on the way to a hospital in a rickshaw when the baby boy was born. The rickshaw coolie decided a visit to hospital was unnecessary as the baby was already delivered, so he brought the woman and child back to camp. The baby was a "blue baby", and the mother was not allowed to take it back out to a hospital, that could not have done anything for the child anyway. Soon the baby died. Generally, when an adult died, there was a funeral service and then the Japanese took the body outside the camp for burial in the British cemetery. This is what the parents decided to ask for; and first the Reverend Hadwen came and conducted a funeral service in their hut. The bereaved parents lived in the next hut to Aunt Haruko, who heard the mother sobbing in the night.

As the winter of 1944 approached, the weather became very cold. The Chinese descriptions, of Cold Dew (Han-lu) for early October and Frost Descent (Shuang-chiang) for the later part of the month, accurately presented this particular season that, in all its damp chill, ushered in the worst winter of our war years. Doreen and I decided to knit a new wardrobe for our dolls; we sat in her family's room, a few doors down from my own, making skirts, jumpers (sweaters) and scarves.

Since we were using odd scraps of wool for this project we tied many knots. As I sat there knitting, several of these knots showed on the right side of my work. Doreen's mother bent over me and used a crochet hook to tweak them through to the back of the garment where they wouldn't show.

Mrs. Hunt no longer taught us Arithmetic as she was expecting a baby and needed the extra rest. She joined us in our knitting sessions – only she was knitting little garments for a real baby. Doreen and her little sister and Isabel and I were all excited anticipating this event. The Hunt girls did all they could to help with cleaning and tidying their living space. Mr. Robertson had negotiated with our camp commandant to obtain a small bottle of milk and some extra food every day for their mother,

In September I had been passed on to another class of older children at the camp school taught by Major Bartley, a schoolteacher and staff major with the Shanghai Volunteer Corps. He was not very tall but gave the impression of height. He had an erect bearing and was always very neatly dressed. His handlebar moustache was in perfect shape, not a hair out of place. I enjoyed doing the arithmetic homework he set and carefully put it into what I thought of as Mrs. Duncan's bag to carry to his class.

We practised our writing by copying the phrase "Necessity is the mother of Invention." I tried, but I could see how messy the work appeared on the page. In all this switching about of classes, no one had formally shown me how to progress from printing to writing. The task of teaching me how to write fell to my brother.

"I don't know how to *write*," I wailed. "Everyone knows how to write except *me*."

"Just draw a line between the letters to join them up," said Gordon practically. This method seemed to work. The teachers did not complain about the way I wrote. I suppose they had other things to bother about.

Under Major Bartley we memorized an incredible amount of military poetry, such as "The Burial of Sir John Moore" and "The Charge of the Light Brigade". He did branch out into a nautical poem starting: "A wet sheet and a flowing sea, a wind that follows fast." We had to pronounce "wind" with a long "i." Major Bartley was even adventurous enough to break away from the mould to have us memorize "I Wandered, Lonely as a Cloud" by William Wordsworth.

As the winter cold came on, and there was no central heating, we wore our coats in school. The wind howled around the camp buildings, and the ground froze stone hard. Sometimes Major Bartley stopped class after half an hour.

"Let's go for a 'canter' to keep warm," he said. In his jodhpurs and polished leather boots he led us on our tour. He had a rather rolling gait. In twos we jogged after him, starting along the field behind the school in G-Block, around T-Camp and the playing field behind B-Block, and coming back to school. I imagined the Major cantering ahead of us on a horse.

We respected him and enjoyed the major's classes. He was strict but humane. He did not go in for the caning that had been common in Gordon's school. Despite his crusty exterior, and the childless state of his marriage, he seemed really to like children.

My brother used his singing abilities in most of our stage productions (not the ballet which he regarded as beneath him as a boy) and for the second Christmas show my mother had promised the producer that Gordon would be the prince to awaken the princess in *Sleeping Beauty*. Before he kissed her awake, Gordon would sing a Gilbert and Sullivan song "When a merry maiden marries."

At first rehearsals went along as usual. But as time passed it became clear that something was the matter with Gordon's part. He was still stumbling over the words after everyone else had learned theirs. He didn't seem to have picked up the tune of his song to the sleeping beauty, never mind the words for it.

Evening after evening our agitated mother sat beside him on one of our beds, taking Gordon through his part, begging him to sing the song. On stage, he scowled and refused to be pleasant to the Sleeping Beauty. These scenes repeated themselves for several weeks of rehearsal until the director asked Gordon why he would not perform.

It turned out he was afraid of his friends' teasing when he awakened the princess with a kiss. Gordon imagined them: a row of tough twelve year old boys, jeering and laughing at him as he kissed the princess to life, making his life miserable with their teasing for weeks after the show was over. The director solved the problem by allowing him to kiss her hand instead.

A very beautiful girl named Galina Cooke played the princess. As my brother grew older, he no doubt regretted his missed opportunity.

That Christmas there were no presents but at breakfast my mother took out the Christmas card our father had made for us. His self-portrait looked thin and anxious, but there was a poem: "Our craft, dear ones, is sailing on, Through mists today, clear seas anon." – and a lovely little decorated evergreen tree drawn on the card. It was the only Christmas tree we had, as there was none anywhere in the camp.

We wished our father could be present. Our mother propped the card on the little table against the wall, where we took our congee, and we pretended that for the moment the portrait was really Daddy, that he truly was there beside us. Gordon and I were immensely cheered at this idea. I thought of my father laughing when he cracked open the hollow egg on our April Fool's Day breakfasts.

After we'd finished, Gordon went to wash our bowls and spoons. I turned to play with the now rather old and crumpled doll's bed, and put my dolls and bear in it. I turned from my playing to see my mother standing by the table. She was stroking the portrait of my father on the card. Then slowly she put the card in its envelope and knelt to put it into the suitcase under her bed. She stayed kneeling by the suitcase for a long time.

There were no pets in our camp, no animals of any kind, and Gordon and I missed and mourned our dogs Janey with her puppy, and Bear. We realized we had no mementoes of them, no photographs – and their collars and licences had been buried with them. But Gordon did have the collar and licence from his adored first dog Dopey, a bulldog.

Because of a boy in our compound we had had a crisis with Dopey. When he came into our garden and threw things and teased and hit Dopey, the dog bit the boy. This happened twice and the ensuing legal case resulted in a death sentence for Dopey – unless he could be found a home on the outskirts of the city where he would be away from people. My father advertised widely round Shanghai and the best reply came from an American businessman, Arnold Kiehn, who had an estate in Hungjao outside the International Settlement for which he wanted a guard dog. Arnold Kiehn was a large genial man.

He came several times to play with our pet. Arnold bravely put out his hand. Dopey came and licked it without hesitation. Arnold got down on the floor and wrestled with Dopey. They took to each other immediately.

So my parents decided to give our pet to Arnold, and we stood sadly on the steps of our house, waving goodbye as Dopey departed in the back seat of Arnold's car, smiling his irrepressible, wide doggy grin at us through the window. As a kind gesture, Arnold Kiehn made a donation in Gordon's name to the Shanghai Society for the Prevention of Cruelty to Animals (SSPCA), large enough to buy Gordon a life membership of the society. Dopey lived with Arnold and died of old age on his estate.

Among the boys in the camp was a bully, a bit older than Gordon. We tended to avoid him. One day this boy stole the collar and licence tag of the dog Gordon had adored. The older boy knew of Gordon's attachment to his pet and that he always carried these things in his pocket.

"Why don't you tell one of the grown-ups on him?" I asked when Gordon told me.

"No, I couldn't do that. I have to fight my own battles. Besides, maybe he'll give them back."

Gordon never did get back the collar and licence. But he had the life membership certificate in our room. We decided that we would not tell anyone about it and that Gordon would not take it out with him or show it to people. This was one possession he had left to remind him of Dopey.

After several absorbing, productive and unusual months under the tutelage of Major Bartley, I was again passed on to a class of older children, run by a trained teacher. She taught us our English and Arithmetic very well, and whacked us over the knuckles with a ruler when she felt like it. I experienced that pain a few times when she hit my hands for talking and laughing in class.

By my third birthday in camp I was nine years old and in the new class. Gordon drew another birthday card and our mother wished me a very happy eighth birthday. Gordon gave me his usual light punch on my arm – and I truly did feel a surge of contentment.

At this time we were now at about two-thirds to half the 1,100 calorie ration of food the Japanese had originally allowed us per day, and stayed in bed in the evenings rather than doing anything but the minimum of other activities. But I still didn't consciously understand the possibility of my own death in our situation.

However, quite early during our stay at Yu Yuen Road I

began to have a recurring nightmare, which was in colour. In the dream, I run to our room to fetch some slippers. They are under a bed. I open the door of our room and notice it looks rather strange. There is a different type of bed there, made of iron, with no bedspread hanging down over the sides; I can easily see underneath. Under the bed I see a pair of slippers. The air is coloured an acid green, with red shading at the edges – and I am terrified. I go to pick up the slippers and I *know* that when I have fully bent down to pick them up someone, standing behind me out of sight, is going to kill me. (I imagine it will be by strangling.) I feel, nevertheless, I must continue. I start bending forward ... and at this point I always woke up, shaking with fear.

I never discussed the nightmare; with the wetting of my bed it seemed a very private trial I must face alone.

21. Human Shields

In China, by early 1945 the Nanking puppet regime was unravelling as its head, Wang Jingwei, had died (some said was murdered) in a Tokyo hospital. His two henchmen were fighting over the succession. The main target for both the Nationalists and Communists was each other. In Shanghai the Japanese had tried unsuccessfully to control the flow of resources such as food. Due to the complicated social and political ties across the boundaries of the occupied and unoccupied areas, the rivalry and corruption of their collaborators and the usual tendency of the Chinese people to go their own way, a substantial underground economy had emerged.

The war was becoming more serious for us prisoners – and the adults, who knew what was happening outside, couldn't help becoming ever more tense: they understood how the Japanese detested losing face, and knew what the Japanese soldiers had already done in China. More personally worrying was the news that before killing themselves Japanese guards were murdering their prisoners. Although, as usual, I wasn't told what was happening, I could feel this tension. It was the same change in atmosphere I had felt before the attack by the Japanese. Our parents were huddling together, and conducted whispered conversations, which would stop when I came near.

With headphones, the designated listener heard a bulletin from Australia summing up the position in the war: By 1945 the Allies were making such headway in North Africa, the Pacific, Italy and the Russian front that they would soon win the war in these areas. In the Far East the situation was becoming more serious for the Japanese. They had found the Chinese war difficult and expensive; but at least they had been winning it and subduing (and murdering) more and more of the Chinese population. However, it was now clear the Japanese could not win...

A tap on the shoulder warned him that a guard was near. The young men turned off the radio and slid it behind the dummy wall, hiding round the corner in the G-Block kitchen. Sounds of boots passing came and then receded. The Japanese were becoming more vigilant. Later the men discussed the unusual presence of a guard inside the buildings at night and the desperate outlook for us as prisoners.

The end of our third April at Yu Yuen Road saw us on the march again to another camp, in the Sacred Heart Convent, which the Shanghai authorities had condemned as unfit for human habitation and the nuns had abandoned. Surrounded by a twelve-foot high wall, this convent was on the outskirts of Shanghai near the Seventh Day Adventist village on Ningkuo Road. Japanese soldiers had been billeted in the convent. They were alarmed at how close Allied bombers were coming, and had decided to switch places with us.

We were there to act as human shields for neighbouring munitions factories and a hospital housing Japanese military patients, which was next to our new camp. Painted on its roof the hospital had a large white cross. It was there to warn the Allied bombers that this was a hospital, not to be bombed under the Geneva Conventions, which the Japanese did not themselves follow.

Once again we packed our belongings. I looked behind the loose brick for my head of the Chinese goddess to find it had gone. When I asked my mother about it, she told me she had thrown it out. I think she objected to it on religious grounds. Although she accepted our servants' religion (for them) my mother didn't like me keeping an icon from that religion for myself. My first thought was to ask where she threw it away so that I could get it back, but she said firmly that the head could not be found again.

I had to accept this fact, and went to pack my toys together with my books, marbles and ball, ready for the journey to our new camp. I put them all in a pillowcase, which I tied at the top. Inside, was the yellow and red bag from Mrs. Duncan containing my books. Everything fitted in nicely except for the blue giraffe. His head came out from the top of the pillowcase as I carried my load to the camp gates.

The women and children were to travel part of the way to the convent by tramcar, carrying whatever they could of their possessions. The men stayed behind and loaded the heavier belongings onto trucks that travelled straight to the camp with the men as well as the baggage.

Guarded by Japanese with bayonets drawn, we walked a few streets round the corner to a long line of trams, waiting to transport the approximately six hundred women and children. I walked along the line with my family and found a carriage that was not yet full. We all climbed in, and found seats. I thought briefly of Amah and the way she always had helped me up onto a tram. But I realized that now I didn't need help. I could do things myself.

I sat on a wooden seat next to a window and put my pillowcase on my knee. In a friendly way the blue giraffe looked out at the road from the top of my toys and books. One after another the trams jerked slowly forward and we were on our way into the outside world for the first time in over three years. The journey was like a strange royal procession. We travelled slowly along main roads cleared of all traffic and lined with a huge crowd of silent Chinese. I looked out of the window, aware of being at the centre of their attention, wondering what they were thinking.

Once a Chinese person broke out of the crowd and ran alongside asking for news of a particular prisoner. There was the scraping of the tram wheels along the lines, but otherwise little broke the eerie silence of our passing. From the trams it looked as if the whole of Shanghai had stopped to watch our transfer. Never before had I seen the city so quiet – and in the middle of the day! The usual *jenao*, hot din, was completely missing.

At the end of the tramline an escort of Japanese on motorcycles, carrying machine guns, came to meet us. They started up their engines in a noisy, threatening way, and fell into line on either side of our column of women and children, weapons at the ready. Then began what seemed to me like a very long march to the convent. My resourceful brother tied as much as he could to a bicycle he had brought along. Those with a free hand helped lead along the very young children among us. Aunt Haruko led a three-year-old Belgian boy named Walter. Everyone helped Mrs. Duncan who was again in pain and couldn't carry anything. The motorcyclists with machine guns guarded and threatened us all the long, burdened, slow, silent way.

To mark our arrival the Allied air force mounted a colossal bombing raid. We had no shelters and the camp leaders advised us to stay indoors. There was a constant din from the endless waves of planes flying low, the bombs shrieking their way down and the dull crash of explosions around the camp. The shock waves from the bombs shook our dilapidated buildings and plaster fell everywhere covering us, and the possessions we had just set out, with a fine dust that we cleared up once daylight came. The Japanese were shooting ineffectually from the grounds of the hospital nearby, with anti-aircraft guns mounted in and around some bushes.

My brother and the Grant boys watched the red-hot pieces of shrapnel and tracer bullets flying about. The bullets left a fiery, dotted trail as they sped to their targets. The boys regarded the whole event as wonderful entertainment. After the raid, Gordon rushed in saying, "Did you see the B-29 superfortresses coming over? We had a great time leaning out of windows to watch the shrapnel go by!" *Leaning out of windows? Shrapnel?* We worried, but it was too late. The air raid was over and no one in the camp had been injured.

This was the first of many, almost daily, air raids around our convent camp, as the Allies pressed in to Shanghai towards the end of the war. They were in touch with local Chinese who always warned the prisoners of bombing raids by throwing messages over the camp wall. The Japanese never knew when a raid was coming. They invariably sounded the air raid warning sirens after most of the bombing was over. The Allied airmen dropped flares for extra visibility, to release their bombs on the right target. This must have helped the Japanese gunners in aiming their bullets towards the planes, adding danger to the bombing raids for the Allies. We never saw an Allied plane go down.

As we faced one raid after another I became increasingly nervous. The bombs dropped close by on the munitions factories. We could see the flames and feel the impact. Parts of the stuccoed fronts of the convent buildings fell off leaving a ragged surface of old brick and grey stucco. The plaster inside cracked, and broke. I was afraid the whole building we were in would collapse. We all suffered from lack of sleep, with its attendant problems of tiredness, nervousness and loss of strength.

I worried that perhaps the Allies would make a mistake and drop a bomb directly on the camp, and began to weigh our chances if the building we occupied fell on top of us. Some people would die; some would lose limbs; others would be trapped under bricks and wood. I decided I'd rather be killed than lose my eyes, and be unable to read any more, or lose my hands and be unable to turn the pages of a book or knit.

It was in this last phase of our internment, then, when I was nine years old that I fully understood that I might never return to the comfortable life I once knew. I gave up longing for the comfortable armchair of our previous existence because it was now forever irrelevant. I did not feel sad or sorry for myself. I did not discuss the matter with my friends or think about it all the time. I just accepted the idea as a fact of my life as it now was. We seemed to have been abandoned. Our old life had vanished and we were living in circumstances for which we had no precedent.

22. This Desolate Place

When we reached the new prison, called Yangtzepoo camp, we found that people from another location, the Columbian Country Club on Great Western Road, had joined us, creating a total of over two thousand. We also had a new commandant, Mr. Hashimoto.

First we went exploring. There was less open space than before. We were entering the period of climate that the Chinese called the Great Heat. Temperatures hovered between 90 and 100 degrees Fahrenheit and humidity was in the high 80s. There were occasional violent storms; the rain seeped down the plaster inner walls of the dilapidated convent buildings leaving brown stains. Outside, water bounced off the parched ground and soon evaporated. What we saw every day was hard, barren mud and, at one end of the camp farthest from the buildings, a stagnant pond.

On the ground floor of each building was a large dormitory, which ran across from end to end. In one of these our family had a space of about eight feet by eight feet. On ropes stretched across from wall to wall, and down the middle, the adults hung sheets for partitions at night. These ropes also provided a place to hang a small bag of weevil-infested porridge we received from the Red Cross parcels as we entered the camp. (My mother rationed out this porridge to us until the end of the war.) Each family looked out onto windowed corridors running the length of the building on either side of the dormitory. At the end of each corridor was a small washroom where we had a washbasin and some running water. Beyond these was a door out to the rest of the camp.

Before our arrival Japanese soldiers occupied the convent – until they decided to change places with us and went to live in the safer (and cleaner) quarters at Yu Yuen Road. They had managed to make all the convent lavatories unusable. Until the plumbers among the prisoners cleared the drains, we used gaps between wood planks placed over a large trench. Using these became a daytime nightmare for me, as I imagined myself falling through the hole I was using into the stinking cesspool below. These facilities were located just outside the corridor into which our own cubicle faced. The stench seeped in through the closed windows. Even after we returned to better sanitary arrangements the smell remained.

Here, the dust storms started. Then, the wind howled for *hours*. Each storm swirled grittily around the camp, holding us prisoner twice over. It created a fog of sand through which we could not see, a wall of wind through which we could not walk, a barrier of sound through which we could not hear. Stale-smelling dust flew through the porous buildings settling on and in everything. We cowered on our beds. It was strange that there were no dust storms when we lived our halcyon, pre-internment camp days just minutes away; but it seemed appropriate that we should be so tormented now. Outside the bushes would be green, and all the fields; but the bushes were dour and dusty, the hard ground dun coloured, here, in this desolate place.

During one of the storms my brother, commenting on information gained from our Children's Encyclopedia (Volume A-D), reminded me of the part about desert Bedouin, who shelter from the wind behind their camels in sandstorms.

"But what about the sand, the *sand*?" I asked.

My brother in a didactic mood said, "Bedouin hide in their flowing robes and pull their long head-dresses over their faces. They're away from the wind, away from the sand and safe."

As I thought about this information I wished *I* had a camel. I imagined it as yellower and neater than the one at the birthday party we'd attended such eons ago, less hairy, and certainly less smelly – not smelly at all! *My* camel (he'd be quite small) would sit sedately in the middle of our dormitory during a dust storm, with me sheltering snugly behind his humps – in my new, blue and white striped Bedouin clothes, just like the ones in the photo of Bedouin in the encyclopaedia (Volume A-D). I could just *feel* myself wearing the new clothes, their solidity and slight roughness against my skin.

In this camp *we* were like Bedouin. We in effect lived in tents: sheets we put up round our cubicles during the night and took down for the day. Given the lack of privacy, I became ever more aware of the people round about than before.

In the cramped, open quarters of the dormitories it

became obvious that one family had more food than the others. The Japanese allowed people from outside, whom the family knew, to send it in. This family occupied the space next to ours in the dormitory. Every day as we contemplated our own dismal day's allowance of one meal of thin congee with a small loaf of sour bread, and another small bowl of cracked wheat issued by the Red Cross, the other mother loudly announced to her children the menu for each meal. "Come along for your corned beef, sweet potatoes, cabbage and carrots. Eat up all your fruit and chocolate pudding," she would say. My mother was angry, but silent.

No doubt heartened by his richer diet, the boy in the next cubicle droned "The Darktown Strutters' Ball" over and over. "We gotta be there whe-en the band starts playin," he crooned loudly as he lay on his bed, in the evening after the partitioning sheets went up, and early in the morning as he woke. At these times I wished I could raise the curtain between the two cubicles, and *crash* my heavy Children's Encyclopædia (Volume A-D) down on that chanting face.

I now had more encyclopaedias to read, thanks to Tony Corner who, with his parents, occupied a cubicle to one side of ours. The Corners were small, neat people. Mr. Corner was a banker and Mrs Corner was a teacher of the deaf.

From my vantage point next to the Corners' space, I listened to Mrs. Corner teaching a little deaf child how to lip-read and speak. Although this was not usual during the day, Mrs. Corner put up the sheet partitions for privacy when she taught the child. He had been going into rages because he couldn't understand what was happening. The other children increasingly thought he was deranged or dangerous. The change in his behaviour after contact with

Mrs. Corner was remarkable. Mrs. Corner told us how to behave with the little boy. We must treat him as an equal human being and speak to him clearly and make sure that he could see and read our lips. From then on his life improved enormously.

In the Corners' son, Tony, I found an interesting new friend. Unlike me, Tony didn't play with the general crowd but had books, which I borrowed, mainly children's encyclopaedias and Edgar Rice Burroughs' stories about Tarzan. I avidly read the stories about "Tarzan the Free," as I came to think of him. Tarzan could swing anywhere using the forest vines. There were no walls for him. He could go swimming whenever he liked, provided he battled the occasional crocodile while in the water.

The new store of books and my obsession with reading them led me into trouble with my mother. We were supposed to put the lights out after dark and keep everything black because of the frequent air raids. However, we had a light with a five watt bulb on a pulley over our cubicle and I read into the night with the light pulled down over the book, shielding it round with my arms so that no light escaped, and I could see without disturbing anyone. This *did* concern my mother who constantly urged me to stop reading. It also bothered me when I started suffering from splitting headaches due to eyestrain, as I still did not have any glasses. I couldn't bear to stop reading, even while suffering one of my headaches.

Tony's other outstanding possession was a magnifying glass. We made a pile of dried grass and paper and Tony said he would harness the power of the sun. Lowering his voice like a magician, Tony said, "Watch carefully. Now, with the glass, I will concentrate the rays of the sun on this pile of dried objects and set it *alight*!" – and he did. The "pile of dried objects" started to smoulder and was quickly burning merrily. We had to scurry smartly about to put out the fire.

Doreen, Isabel and I joined a new Brownie troop that had been set up. We didn't have the energy to do anything very active, but sat round in a circle with the other members of our "six" (I was the "sixer") contentedly tying knots.

On one of our Brownie days, in June 1945, Doreen's little sister came to tell us that their mother had gone to hospital to have the baby. And the next morning Doreen came to tell me they had a new brother.

He came back with Mrs. Hunt the following afternoon and Isabel, Doreen and I gathered round his cot to admire him. We wanted to know when we could play houses – with him as the baby. Mrs. Hunt said he was too fragile just now and that it would be a year or two at least before we could play with him like that. So we went back to our dolls: not alive, but sturdy.

To give the children something to do, some priests put up two parallel bars, with wood supporting a length of pipe. They taught us to do various exercises. Most of the children left the bars alone, but I developed calluses on my hands from (a perhaps rather obsessive) swinging. I swung back and forth pretending I was flying. In a kind of trance, I saw myself travelling in the air above the camp like Tarzan the Free, flying over the wall to be with Amah at her home in Canton. I imagined us sitting in her family kitchen, which would be like the one on Bubbling Well Road. Amah would take me on her knee and feed me delicious rice and vegetables from her own bowl, and give me cake, and stroke my hair.

I felt like the bird I had once seen, struggling to free itself from an immensely strong web. An enormous spider had spun it outside a landing window of the hotel in Wei Hai Wei, in north China, where we sometimes went on holiday. My brother had rescued the bird; I wondered who would rescue me.

23. Life at Ningkuo Road

Our new camp was on Ningkuo Road near the village where we had lived before, and at the end of the camp farthest away from the buildings, was a stagnant pond, a possible breeding ground for mosquitoes carrying malaria. The adults worried about an epidemic. So did the Japanese who, concerned about their own health, had us vaccinated against the disease. Sometimes summer thunder accompanied the rainstorms, and I thought of Amah and Bubbling Well Road...

It was raining with thunder outside our house at Bubbling Well Road. Amah and I were sitting close together hugging the dog, Janey, who was frightened by the noise. We had just come in from a walk and had brought home some roasted chestnuts from a roadside brazier. Amah removed the shells and we sat together in front of the fire, eating the delicious soft nuts, in a safe world of our own...

A few weeks later, after the annual spring flood, my brother and I went, as usual, to a local pet store to buy a tortoise each. We gazed down at tortoises of various sizes, swimming about in a huge, earthenware Soochow tub standing on the floor. The glazed tub, large enough for an adult to bathe in, was white on the inside and dark brown outside. My brother always chose the biggest tortoise he could find and I always chose the smallest.

The creatures lived with us in a specially built home until autumn when we released them in the garden. There they dug themselves into the mud of a flowerbed to hibernate until spring. There was one large one in particular which returned to us each spring floating on top of the floodwater.

I spent increasing amounts of time in my dream world. Swinging back and forth on the parallel bars, I escaped into a kind of trance, and willed myself back to happier times when we were on holiday …

As a very small toddler I stand in the edge of the sea watching a school of small fish as they make a silvery dart between my legs in the crystal water. I wonder how such small creatures can dare to swim so close to someone as large as myself. On the same holiday I am dogpaddling about, surrounded by a circle of women: my mother and her friends. They are clad in fine, machine knitted bathing suits and as I go from one to another I grasp on to the belts of the suits.

It seemed to me there were two worlds in which I lived as a child. There was the world of the large where the child is very small and adults are the right size, and there was the world of the small, where the child is the right size and everything else relates to that size. The tiny fish inhabited the small world and so too did Amah. I thought this was because she had a habit of squatting down and looking me in the eyes at my level when she talked to me.

Increasingly, as well as daydreaming, reading became my escape. I no longer had the energy to play with large groups of other children. There was less leisure time anyway as now we children had to go to school all day. Doreen Hunt, Isabel Gomersall and I did not see each other as much as before. I do not remember being in the same classes with them, and there were no more special extra lessons in which we learned as a group. My bag was becoming rather worn and there was a hole in one corner from which part of a book would protrude. My studies expanded to include French and Latin.

The supplies from our previous school internment camp were running out. We had to use our writing paper several times. We wrote lightly in pencil and then erased. A group of us got into trouble for spreading out our writing to obtain a new piece of paper sooner.

For me the highlight of this camp's schooling was reading and discussing with our class "The Lady of Shalott" by Tennyson. One boy managed to find a large sheet of blank paper and, inspired by the poem, produced a magnificent drawing of the "Four gray walls, and four gray towers" of the Lady's castle prison on the island of Shalott. Our teacher hung it up for all of us to enjoy.

In this camp Mrs. Duncan's pain again became severe. My mother also had many bouts of pain from her gall bladder and was often in bed. Mrs. Corner stayed with her and gave her drinks of water until the attacks passed. I heard Mrs. Corner say to another prisoner that she was afraid my mother's gall bladder would burst. I did not know what to do to help, and wondered whether my mother would die.

I did not discuss my fears and didn't even ask whether this gall bladder problem was life threatening. My thoughts included concerns about our father. We had no more letters from him. We did have information through the local Chinese over-the-wall intelligence that the Haiphong Road prisoners had gone towards north China, either for extermination or (ultimately the same fate) for transportation to Japan as slave labourers. First, however, they would act as human shields for Japanese troops crossing to Japan. Of course, no one told me these details at the time.

We found out later that prisoners of our father's internment camp left from Shanghai by rail in cattle trucks on July 8, 1945. For four days they traveled north, in cramped conditions, with very little food and no water except what the Japanese allowed them to snatch where possible at infrequent stops. The sanitary arrangements during the journey were vile. Many suffered from dysentery. Everyone had swollen feet and ankles from the crowded conditions and lack of movement.

After leaving the train the men marched over a stony road for a mile or two to Fengtai, about eight miles south of Peking, where the Japanese used their rifle butts to push them into dirty wooden godowns (warehouses) – again with no lavatories or running water. (China, as a great trading nation, has many godowns in which to store goods moving within China from intra-Chinese trade or from foreign markets.) There the prisoners sweltered for over four weeks, packed in at 180 men per godown. They were not allowed out to exercise or wash themselves.

And so I worried – and wondered what might happen to Gordon and me if our parents both died.

Our food ration was cut again. By May it was down to one "meal" a day from the Japanese, the meal consisting of a ladle of watery congee. The food allocated came to 300 calories, and Red Cross relief parcels were often not distributed to us.

I was becoming quite weary. There were too many excruciating headaches from eyestrain and too many bouts of illness. My first sickness at the new camp was another jaundice attack. The illness did prompt our camp doctor to order my family moved to a room upstairs. This gave us more space and, above all, privacy – and freedom from the stench of the old cesspool below.

However, the room we now had was infested with cockroaches, which I had not noticed in the dormitory. The cockroaches scurried through the many crevices in the plaster and gathered in large numbers at night, forming seething black patches on the walls. As my eyesight was becoming worse I couldn't see the cracks in the plaster. My brother told me about them.

Some prisoners, including myself, suffered bouts of dengue fever, a strange illness that makes the sufferer feel incredibly cold even on the hottest summer day. We shivered, covered with all the blankets and coats our relatives could muster. These cold feelings alternated with hot, feverish spells. Still there were no drugs or hospital care available.

During these fevered times, the cockroaches became even more bold than usual and I imagined (or really did see) huge ones sitting silently on the blankets of my bed, watching, and waiting. *Are they waiting for me to become so weak they will be able to crawl all over me?* I wondered, and shuddered at the thought. To get away from their malevolent presence I sometimes got up and went to my mother and her friends, sitting chatting outside in deck chairs.

From our higher window we were able to see over the convent wall into the grounds of the hospital and barracks. At our new vantage point my brother and I could see the details of what was happening across the road.

We could see all Japanese military patients who were not confined to bed being drilled at early morning exercises until some of them collapsed. The drillmaster shouted and kicked at the fallen men until they fainted or somehow managed to stand up again. These exercises took place twice a day. As soon as a man could stand, even with bandages on, he was made to exercise. In this way my brother and I saw at first hand some of the brutalizing of the Japanese troops, a policy that created a fighting force that behaved particularly cruelly to its victims. At the other end of the parade ground from the hospital were barracks for Japanese soldiers.

The camp radio pull toy truck, which was in full view of the Japanese at times, came with us to Ningkuo Road. From this the prisoners had heard the news of the surrender of Germany and the proclamation of V-E Day (Victory in Europe Day) on May 8, 1945. The Allies asked for peace from the Japanese, pointing out it was a matter of time before they lost the Pacific war, but Emperor Hirohito sent a defiant reply. The prisoners waited in some fear for the inevitable Japanese collapse. The adults asked themselves what these people, with their belief in committing suicide rather than be taken alive, would do – with themselves and with their prisoners. Mr. Robertson's exceptional skills in communicating with the Japanese became crucial. Now his mission, to get as many prisoners as possible out of the war alive, was becoming increasingly important. The food situation was dire and the Japanese said their cash allowance bought less and less due to inflation. So the Swiss took over and made bulk deliveries to the camps in June and July, a move that averted starvation for those unable to obtain relief from friends outside. But August came with no further food relief.

In our internment camp the Japanese carried out plans that they said were for defence of the camp by the guards if there was an Allied invasion. In late July they forced some male prisoners to dig trenches that they said were for the guards to use to fight from – but there were far more than the small number of guards could occupy by themselves. Several times my mother mentioned to me the reason given for digging the trenches and also the oddly large number of them. I sensed they made her nervous. I noted my mother's concern, enough to remember it, but I did not think much about this matter at the time.

By August, news of the war in the Far East was good for the Allies. At Ningkuo Road there was a general air of tension and waiting, waiting for what fate would hand out. Lack of food made people less energetic and many were ill. My mother continued to have painful gall bladder attacks. Aunt Haruko, suffering from a nervous breakdown, sat shaking on her bed. Among many prisoners, weak from the lack of food and from illness, there was an unconscious, gradual withdrawal, a listless turning away from living towards dying.

In Fengtai, where my father was held prisoner, all the men were beaten with rifle butts and forced to pack into one godown. The Japanese then sprayed petrol over the whole of the outside surface of the godown. For over an hour the prisoners waited. Herding people into a building and setting it alight was a favourite way for the Japanese to murder Chinese civilians. Now it could be the turn of the foreign prisoners. There was a pause as the Japanese discussed what to do. The guards surrounded the godown and drew their guns, to be ready to shoot anyone who tried to escape.

24. The Gang of Three

Now thirteen, my brother Gordon continued to mend shoes with Abe Abraham, as he had at Yu Yuen Road. They set themselves up in a professional way in a little "shop" at one side of the camp. The Red Cross had now sent in cobblers' tools and rectangular pieces cut from rubber tires, which the boys cut to size and sewed on to the upper parts of shoes in need of repair. Other people with practical skills, such as electricians and carpenters, were available in two other shops along the same side of the camp beside the cobblers. The row of small buildings was completed by a bathhouse for the Japanese guards.

In his spare time Gordon, ragged and in bare feet, roamed around with two other boys, Kenneth Crichton and Ronnie Colman. There was no listless turning away from living for them. "Both of them would steal anything," said Gordon. They explored the camp and knew every place where they could get rope or nails or odd pieces of wood. The boys scrounged what they needed to make a raft. They went to the pond at the edge of the camp and punted around, raced other rafts, observed the pond's frogs and had imaginary adventures. They also managed to find a little extra food, and get up to mischief. The boys knew that victory for the Allies was near and Gordon forgot Mr. Robertson's stern lecture about not annoying the Japanese.

At about sunset every evening the Japanese guards took a bath in very hot water contained in congs (very deep metal tubs) heated from below by fires. They lit the fires, left them to heat the water and then returned to have baths when the water was hot, first extinguishing the fires. The "Gang of Three" had the bright idea of stealing into the bathhouse when the guards were away and playing a trick on them. Gordon told me not to tell anyone, but to watch the bathhouse from an upstairs window. I saw the boys creep in carrying handfuls of mud, which they threw into the heating water. They then hid upstairs with me and we watched to see the result.

Like the shops in the same row, the bathhouse was open on one side. Along came the guards. They looked forward to their bath after a day working in the hot and humid Shanghai weather. The Japanese stripped and settled gratefully into the hot water – only to realize there was something in there with them. They jumped out, saw the mess they were in, and went wild. Clad in towels the guards rushed out looking for the culprits. The boys laughed madly and as silently as they could.

I worried about what the guards would do in revenge. The Japanese had lost face but said nothing. Mr. Robertson worried about consequences.

From the window of our room Gordon and his friends could see across the wall to the barracks. They noticed that some of the equipment for the soldiers was left lying around in boxes outside. They watched the Japanese soldiers cooking on small cans (about three inches or eight centimetres in diameter) of what looked like wax. When they needed to cook they lit the wax with a match, and put the lid on the can to extinguish the fire: Simple.

Gordon had been helping our mother when she wanted to cook porridge in the evening on a little hot plate we had. He had to clamber onto a bed. Then he removed the light bulb and connected the hot plate wire to the light. He often went reeling around afterwards with an electric shock from a bad connection. Gordon and his friends decided to steal something from the Japanese. Given Gordon's experiences with trying to plug in our hot plate, they thought the best thing to steal was the Canned Heat, as we all came to call it.

As it was cooler there, I had been sleeping in the corridor outside our room and soon became aware of some nocturnal wanderings. One night Gordon padded past my bed. His face was covered with mud and he was on his way to the washroom to clean himself.

"What are you doing, where have you been?" I whispered.

"We've been on a stealing expedition. The Japanese guards and soldiers aren't expecting anyone to take their goods. Kenneth and Ronnie and I went over the wall, slithered in the dark to the soldiers' stores and pocketed a few cans. They were lying close to the wall in boxes. It was easy."

"Cans of what?"

"That stuff they use to cook with."

"Where are you going to keep them?"

"Under my bed."

"Oh well, just make sure you don't wake up Mummy. She'll be worried." And I went back to sleep.

However the boys couldn't leave it at that. After stealing a few cans they became more ambitious, and taking a basket with them, they filled it with cans and managed to climb back over the wall undetected by the sentries on patrol. By this time the boys were thoroughly enjoying the adventure. I even provided storage under my bed. The cans didn't really make too much difference as I had my books, clothes and marbles and ball under there already. I became quite accustomed to the nightly wanderings. Gordon was so quiet I was hardly aware of them.

The boys became even more obsessed with their stealing expeditions. (This was the best fun they had had in a long time.) They planned an ambitious raid in which they would take a whole *box* of Canned Heat. They had tried lifting the boxes, which were heavy, so they would need a strong rope to tie up the box and lift it over the wall. The boys went around the camp and found a good thick rope in a shed the Japanese guards used, and hid it to take with them on the next expedition. Gordon told me they were going to do something really big in the middle of the night. I'd see the result in the morning.

That night the Gang of Three stole away from their rooms when everyone else was asleep, found a box of Canned Heat and tied the rope around it. Between them they had no trouble carrying the box to the wall and positioning themselves before starting to haul it over. One boy was on the camp side of the wall pulling. Another sat on top of the wall guiding the rope and the third (Gordon) pushed the box up from the outside. All went well until they had the box about half way up.

Everything was quiet, with the wall in deep shadow,

when suddenly the boys heard a guard on duty, pacing on his round. They froze in mid action. Gordon silently slid behind a bush. Their luck held and the guard paced by without noticing.

When the boys finished they fell about, doubled over with suppressed laughter. This was the best raid yet, and they now had enough Canned Heat for everyone who might want some. Gordon, Kenneth and Ronnie hid the cans under their beds and put some more under mine. After morning roll call Gordon told me what had happened. I hadn't been awake at all that night.

They now went public with their Canned Heat and distributed the cans to whoever would like to have them. The anxious parents told their sons not to go on any more dangerous stealing expeditions. Our mother had a long talk with Gordon about the consequences for us all if he were caught stealing. She pointed out that our father would not be pleased.

Soon the prisoners were cooking their weevily porridge out in the open as it was dangerous to use Canned Heat indoors. They tried to do it without the guards noticing, but the Japanese found out and looked very annoyed. They would lose face by asking who had stolen the cans. They had lost face already by having them stolen and flaunted in the open.

So the soldiers in the barracks outside decided to lay a trap: they placed low, creaky, bamboo beds all around the storage boxes of Canned Heat. They took out some of the cans and placed them in inviting piles around the inner circle beyond the beds. Looking out of our window, the boys saw the preparations. To steal some more cans would now be an even *more* daring adventure. It would take cunning and skill, audacity and courage. The enemy knew in advance the cans might be stolen and the boys were dying to try another raid.

For three weeks the gang of three watched the barracks. They couldn't resist the challenge and decided to make one last, dangerous raid to show they could do it. The action was not only risky, it was also needless as by now the internees had enough cans for what little cooking they were able to do.

After a few more days of inaction to lull the Japanese soldiers into a false sense of security, the boys made their move. In the darkest hours of the night Gordon and his friends crept out of bed after their families were asleep. They had all been to films before being interned and had seen spies or burglars preparing for raids. The boys again plastered mud over their faces, and this time over their arms and legs, for camouflage as seen in these pre-camp films, and climbed warily to the top of the wall. They dropped silently over. Each carrying a basket, the teenagers crawled into the storage area, taking advantage of cover from the dark and the long grass until they reached the bamboo beds. There were no soldiers about, and very carefully, the boys were able to slide through the bamboo barrier and load their baskets with cans. The difficulty came on the way back.

As they crawled under the bamboo beds there came one loud creak from several beds away from the boys. Almost immediately a Japanese soldier burst out brandishing his bayonet and shouting the battle cry, "Banzai." He ran over, shining a torch, looking slowly through beds and parting the grass with his weapon. The boys lay still, trying not to breathe too deeply, in a cold sweat, waiting for the thrust and then twist of steel in their bodies. Eventually the soldier decided nobody was there and walked away. But the boys waited a long time before finally moving, afraid now that dawn would catch them on the wrong side of the camp wall. Once safely back they had another delighted, backslapping session, suppressing their laughter.

In one corner of the camp was a pigsty, for a pig donated by the Red Cross for fattening: another mouth for the camp to feed. (The Red Cross did not seem fully to understand our dire shortage of food.) The boys decided to sink the stolen cans safely out of sight in the pig's swill and went to bed. They could think of a more permanent hiding place later.

Gordon washed in the cold water from the wash hand basin at the end of the corridor. I woke up and saw him as he slipped into bed in our room – as before careful not to wake up our mother. At once he fell into the sleep of the relieved, the exhausted and the satisfied, congratulating himself on the latest successful exploit.

In the early morning I woke up again to see an agitated Ronnie Colman padding silently along the corridor in his bare feet. Ronnie slid into our room leaving the door open. He shook Gordon awake and beckoned him to come out. As Gordon pulled on his clothes Ronnie whispered that he had just been to check on the cans – and had found them floating, bobbing around on top of the pig's swill. *Crisis.* Gordon and Ronnie rushed out along the corridor and down the stairs. I decided to get dressed myself. Off I went after them walking quietly, and putting on my sandals when I reached the outside door. I rounded the corner to the sty just in time to see Gordon and Ronnie putting straw, from a shed behind the sty, over the cans just as people were beginning to wake up and walk about. *Relief.*

Seeing me, they asked me to keep watch while they took each messy can and buried it under the straw in the shed. I sat on top of the fence and let them know when anyone was coming. At last, can by slippery can, the boys finished their task.

"That's what we should have done in the first place," said Ronnie.

"Okay, so you're so clever," said Gordon, "Why didn't you say so at the time?"

Turning to go back to our rooms, we met the first of the men who made our food. He was going to start the congee for breakfast. "Good morning. You're up early," he said as he walked past. "Good morning," chorused Ronnie and Gordon, leaning nonchalantly (they hoped) on the fence of the sty. Sweaty and dirty, the boys washed in time for morning roll call, and went back to their daily round determined to pretend they had just got up having had a good night's sleep.

After this escapade the guards looked even more annoyed. They had been beaten. The thieves had escaped their trap.

At about the same time as the Canned Heat and Mud Bath incidents, there was the Liquor Affair. The camp's commandant had a suite of rooms in the administration block. There was a drainpipe down the building and a ledge running along below all the windows. One of the other, older boys waited until Mr. Hashimoto was out, and climbed up the drainpipe. He crawled along the ledge, entered the commandant's room by the window and stole three bottles of liquor, returning the same way he had come.

The stolen liquor was the last straw. The Japanese had organized their prisoners into groups, with one person in each responsible for the good behaviour of the rest. Mr. Robertson was expected to account for the camp as a whole and received an enraged lecture from the Commandant, who ordered the whole camp to assemble in the area in front of the administration block. He announced there would be severe reprisals if the culprits of the Canned Heat, Mud Bath and Liquor affairs, and the liquor, were not handed over by the next day, when he would call another full camp assembly.

25. The Last Week

The last week of the war began with waves of light, which washed in eerie silence over the camp. Some said the light was brighter than the sun shining outside. It surged and receded in waves for a few moments, and then it was gone. I was no doubt listlessly looking at a book I was reading, our Children's Encyclopaedia (Volume A-D), and missed the event. The encyclopaedia was becoming rather grubby and crumpled from so much use. Visions of armadillos and Archimedes, bats and Babylonia, dragonflies and Demosthenes, filled my head – a welcome relief from the bare mud outside and the cracked walls around me.

From the secret radio the prisoners learned that the Allies, tired of war and Japan's refusals of peace, had dropped very powerful bombs on Hiroshima and Nagasaki. The glare from Nagasaki may have travelled almost 500 miles across the sea to Shanghai. The joint immediate death toll was 120,000 – less than one-half the number of Chinese murdered manually by the Japanese in Nanking alone. Of course, we must mourn each and every death. Hiroshima and Nagasaki were the tragic consequence, for Japanese civilians, of their government's decisions.

We later found out that after the Japanese had refused

requests to surrender, after the Potsdam Conference ending on August 2, 1945, President Truman asked for estimates of the death toll should the war continue by conventional means. Bearing in mind battles such as Saipan and Iwo Jima, the estimate came back of about 4 million Allied troops and 17 million Japanese over about 18 months. Then, to end the war as soon as possible, Truman decided to drop the atomic bombs on August 6, and 9, each time warning the Japanese in advance and asking again for peace, and each time receiving a defiant negative from Emperor Hirohito. And so the Japanese civilians died.

In the next few days Mr. Robertson spent tense hours buying vital time, reasoning with our captors who, nervous about news of the war, and incensed at the tricks played on them, were looking for revenge. Mr. Robertson managed some delay, but by the second week of August our commandant gave the worrying ultimatum: the culprits or else. On the next day everyone gathered. Neither my mother nor I went to the assembly. She was ill and by then I stayed with my mother virtually all the time. I reasoned that if I watched over her, my mother would not die.

The camp was silent. The air hung, heavy and humid. Suddenly we heard a great shout. Then people were cheering. Gordon burst in to tell us that Mr. Robertson had announced the end of the war and the peaceful surrender of Japan and of our guards.

After the announcement, we stayed in the camp, waiting. Day and night, thousands of refugees, ragged, exhausted, jubilant, streamed past on the road to the centre of Shanghai. They called to us to come out; the war was over; we were free. One Russian woman shouted so loudly urging us to leave that one of the guards, enraged, beat her. Mr. Hashimoto came to her rescue.

Our food supply was even worse than before. Everyone used up any reserve they had. My mother rationed out to herself and Gordon a tin of corned beef she had kept, and gave me a tin of fruit – as I refused to eat the corned beef. We had no news of our father, and this became the main worry for my mother, Gordon and me. During this time I continued my swinging on the parallel bars, and each swoop contained the same thought: *Is he safe … Is he safe … Is he safe?*

In the meantime Mr. Robertson's group drew up a letter, signed by most former prisoners, urging clemency for our guards and commandant. Thanks to a brilliant liaison led by Robertson, who was fifty-four years of age at the war's end, we had had more decent treatment than other camps. This was true, but the letter was also possibly a placatory move. After all, the guards and also the soldiers in the nearby barracks were still fully armed. No one had yet arrived to rescue us.

Remarkably, throughout the increasingly dire circumstances of their imprisonment during the war, prisoners of all the Shanghai internment camps continued with their routine of camp duties, the education of their children, their family lives and sense of community. Even more remarkably, in the limbo that developed after the end of war, this order and discipline continued.

At the war's end, we at our camp seemed to be in a little isolated world, still guarded by the Japanese. We wondered when someone was going to come and release us. Some Allied officials did visit us on August 21, with food.

In a few days the United States air force B29s came over again. They swooped down low over the camp, and my heart went cold. *Surely they were not going to start bombing again. And surely not us.* They couldn't be making the mistake I had feared all along. (After all a Japanese military camp was just over the wall.) But surely now that the war was over we would not die – and by the action of our friends.

Then the bomb doors opened, huge metal containers fell and their parachutes ballooned out. They drifted down towards the pond. I wondered whether they were some new kind of bomb and braced myself for the impact. But when they reached the ground out fell all sorts of food. Some containers fell inside the camp near the pond and others outside where, ironically, they killed several Chinese trying to catch the heavy canisters.

That miraculous rain of food from the sky! The containers burst open, showering out a glorious harvest of chocolate bars (thick and strong enough to feed a soldier for a whole day's march), rich cold cereal complete with cream (just add water), cans of meat, dried eggs, corn, honey, vegetables, condensed milk and fruit, jam, concentrated fruit and nut bars, chewing gum … and on and on. We all ran to pick up the packets.

Someone gave me a concentrated fruit and nut bar, which I hesitantly ate and promptly vomited back. Strangely, I didn't feel all that hungry. My starvation had gone beyond hunger. My mother had to start urging me to eat all over again, just like before we went into the camps.

On August 26, two weeks after the Peace was signed, a jeep arrived with two American soldiers in it. One, Bob Schiller, looked like an old-fashioned buccaneer. He was festooned with rifles and swords taken from the Japanese. Schiller clanked cheerfully along and took the surrender. He piled up the back of the jeep with even more swords, guns and rifles. Later came twenty-seven American doctors fanning out among the camps to provide medical care and advice.

Slowly and cautiously, we walked out of the gates of our camp, illogically expecting any minute to be shot by the former guards. After a few days I went with my mother and Mrs. Grant to check on our flat at the Seventh Day Adventists' village nearby. We arrived just in time to see Chinese Nationalist soldiers removing all our furniture. They said they were only borrowing.

With the opening up of the camp, peddlers, belonging to all the nationalities gathered in pre-war Shanghai, flooded in looking for goods to barter, buy and sell. Not daunted, Gordon, Kenneth and Ronnie retrieved the Canned Heat from the pig sty, cleaned up the cans and bartered them for bars of chocolate, (two cans for one bar of chocolate). It was an amazing time.

First the American forces took over with great generosity and kindness. Individual GIs befriended the children, telling them stories. We felt taken up in the strong arms of friends. They brought movies. The first one I recall was *Meet Me In St. Louis* shown outdoors on a large screen set up in the square in front of the administration building where the internees had heard about the end of the war. Rain poured down, but we didn't mind. I became an instant fan of the other Margaret (O'Brien) who played a part in the movie. A group of Chinese businessmen gave each of us 80,000 dollars of the new currency issued by the

211

Nationalists' Central Reserve Bank. Peddlers sold us, or bartered, lollipops and chocolate to enjoy during the movie. I spent all my money on a lollipop and a small painted wooden brooch in the shape of a tortoise. This new life seemed so luxurious.

Returning to my father and his companion captives, when the Japanese at Fengtai had prepared to burn their prisoners alive, there was a lengthy pause and shouting. Cooler heads among the guards prevailed and after an argument lasting over half an hour the Japanese pulled out the nails. The building doors opened, and the men went slowly back to their own godowns.

Further weakened by this ordeal, many began to lose all hope. They wondered when the Japanese would find an opportunity to finish the job. My father wrote that, "… in the last days our fates were in the lap of the Gods."

A few days after this near murder of the prisoners, on August 18, the guards ordered them to get up late at night and pack their belongings. The men thought this was the end for them. They were forced to walk some distance along the road to Peking, but many collapsed unable to go on. The Japanese then requisitioned some trucks for transport. They finally told their prisoners the war was over, and that they were being taken to Peking to meet up with what the Allies had named the United Nations Mission, which was taking over former prisoners. This new situation was difficult to take in. The men discussed among themselves the reason for the move, and decided they were really being taken to Peking to avoid the United Nations Mission people seeing the cruel and filthy conditions in their camp – and at night to avoid loss of face before the Chinese.

And then the prisoners found themselves in the middle of a magical happening. As the trucks travelled towards the city, at about 1 a.m. on August 19, they saw flickering lights. The roadside was filled with hundreds of thousands of Chinese. They stood many deep for at least a mile along the way, lighting the way with candles. The Chinese lined the route to the hotel where the prisoners were being taken, filling the sidewalk, spilling out onto the road; and they clapped and shouted "Hau," in acknowledgement and welcome to the former prisoners, to the strangers coming to their city. Chinese people threw into the trucks fruit and cigarettes for the former prisoners. They ran alongside to shake hands.

Author's Note

I have received two somewhat different accounts of the Japanese guards' decision not to burn alive my father's group of prisoners. One was that the people of Fengtai village pled on their behalf. The other that among the guards was a Chinese speaking element from Formosa, who reasoned against the murder. What seems clear, is that Chinese voices were raised to preserve the lives of my father and his fellow prisoners. I send them my heartfelt gratitude.

PART III
RELEASE

WARTIME CHINA
AND
JAPAN / THE PACIFIC

USSR

MANCHURIA

Peking

Wei Hai Wei

NORTH
KOREA

SOUTH
KOREA

Sea
of
Japan

Hiroshima

Yellow
Sea

Nanking

Nagasaki

Yangtze River

Shanghai

Formosa
(Taiwan)

Hong Kong

26. Reunion

On October 11, 1945, when the USS Lavaca bringing the Haiphong Road men to Shanghai docked, we were still in the convent camp, as we had no money and were safer there for the meantime. (The Chinese banks automatically converted any money transferred from abroad into worthless local currency and all foreign banks were forbidden to function in China.) When our father came, Gordon and I raced along the corridor of the upper storey of our building to meet him. My brother said he looked a lot older and thinner, but to me he looked perfect. My mother, radiant despite her illness, went forward for him to hug her. For a long time my father held my mother very close. It reminded me of the evening when he had come in with the letter from Major Bourne. Only this occasion was a happy one.

At about the same time, Ah Fok and Ah Ling arrived. They had gone from camp to camp until they found us. They gave us all big hugs and I spent many happy hours with Amah catching up on what I was doing now and roaming around outside the camp with her. Amah was surprised when I firmly refused to allow her to wash and dress me any more.

We went together to the Chinese quarter of Nantao and wandered through the narrow lanes looking for a souvenir for me to buy. Amah and I walked under washing the Chinese had strung over the lanes. We saw people gathered round a tap in the middle of a lane gossiping together and fetching water in jugs. It was all so normal, so peaceful. One singsong girl, like the ones we had seen on our way to church (it seemed so long ago) was sitting outside a house painting her toenails ready for her evening's work. Amah said most of the singsong girls came from Soochow, a place known throughout China for the beauty of its women and their pretty, lilting speech. They were rather like French courtesans and could converse on current affairs and play musical instruments.

Everywhere there was the typical busyness of the people of Shanghai. There was a strong Buddhist presence in all the streets, where there were small statues of Buddha in between the shops. As they hurried past the Chinese lightly touched the Buddhas. Nearby the famous Huxingting (Heart-of-Lake Pavilion) tea-house rose in the middle of a lake, and customers entered by a bridge with nine zig-zags (to ward off evil spirits, which can only fly straight). Already beggars, forbidden under Japanese rule, had stationed themselves in the angles of the bridge.

Down one lane a middle-aged man was haggling with the butcher's wife over some meat. Amah said he was also complaining to the shopkeeper about his wife and father-in-law. Amah told me the lanes were narrow and dark, but the houses faced inward round a courtyard where light came in. Over a wall we could hear Chinese music from a gramophone, and people talking and calling to each other.

We went to a laneway with many stalls where soapstone carvers sat working on the floor with their finished carvings around them. At last I found, and Amah bought, that special little soapstone carving – of a boy playing a flute.

On this outing Amah also took me to see the Chenghuang Miao, Temple of the City God. This temple, one of many in Shanghai, was the centre of local festivals and flower shows; it was surrounded by vendors of incense and brightly coloured paper spirit money, food and tea stalls, tea-houses and specialized stalls selling all manner of goods from kitchen wares to textiles.

On another day, my father and I went out to find a Chinese cloth doll. The one I chose was about three feet high and had on silk clothes and a dark silk domed hat to match. As we walked away with our prize, the Chinese we passed were all laughing and calling out to my father who was smiling at them.

"Daddy, what do the Chinese people find so funny?" I asked. "They're asking why I've allowed you to buy a doll dressed as an old man." But I was content. The doll reminded me of our school's major domo, Mr. Lo.

"I want you to see as much as possible of Shanghai before we return to Britain," said our father one day. "You will probably never again see a city that is so modern, cosmopolitan and vibrant as this one." So by pedicab we took a tour of a number of buildings that my father said were built in the art deco style.

Among them was the house of the feared and admired gangster and community leader Du Yuesheng. It was on the French Concession's Rue Wagner where he had lived with his three wives (one on each floor) nine cars, eighteen chauffeurs, three bodyguards and many servants. My father told us that Du showed displeasure with anyone by sending them a coffin. While we were in the French Concession we also went to see the six-floored Great World amusement palace at Avenue Edouard VII and Tibet Road. It was owned by Du's henchman, Huang Jinrong, or "Pockmarked Huang". My father didn't take us in, saying there was a lot of gambling and some not very nice people there. He pointed out an opening on the sixth floor where, if you had spent all you had, you could jump off.

Until we left Shanghai Ah Fok and Ah Ling came every day to look after us. Early in the morning they even brought us *dahping,* a heavenly fried bread, with savory pancakes. We had a tranquil and happy time together living as a family again until my mother could have the gall bladder operation she so badly needed.

Our father was obviously glad to see Gordon and me, and after his return he and our mother went into the same close little world they had inhabited before the attack on the International Settlement. Their closeness to each other did not make me feel excluded but created a feeling of safety. There were no more worries about one or both of them dying.

At night after I was in bed I could sometimes hear them talking quietly. I heard what had happened to one of the men at Haiphong Road. When another man, instead of him, was mistakenly accused of sending messages outside the camp, this man owned up. The Japanese took him to Bridge House jail and rotating teams of guards badgered, and beat him with clubs. When he became maddened, possibly brain-damaged, and unruly, from the mistreatment, they trussed him up tightly with ropes for four days leaving him out in the sun with no water or food – and kept him awake for days. At last the Japanese soldiers brought their prisoner back to Haiphong Road. As he lay on his bed: a sobbing, groaning, bleeding mass, unable to move, he started to sing softly. The scarcely audible song drifted out to the growing group of prisoners gathering silently beside the bed. It was "When Irish Eyes are Smiling" over and over … and then the singing stopped. His name was William Hutton and he died soon after.

I knew my parents didn't want me to hear about something so violent, so tragic, happening, so I didn't say anything to them. I thought it was terribly sad, and his wife and children having to know about it, how their loved father-husband had died.

Soon after the war ended our old study group went to visit Isabel Gomersall. Her father was staying to wind up his business interests, but Isabel, her mother and sisters were going to Britain. We had lunch in the magnificent dining room she had described to us, sitting at one end of the long table. Mr. Gomersall presided over the lunch, although he placed me at the head of the table and himself to my right. Doreen Hunt and Isabel sat to my left.

When we first started our special study group, I was annoyed with Isabel for constantly "boasting" about the house and especially the large dining room she had left behind, a dining room seating eighteen or twenty people. Now, as we had lunch, I realized that these reminiscences about the dining room were for Isabel what my longing for the comfortable armchairs were for me. She had been homesick.

221

British Armed Forces took over our camp and unlike the Americans began to charge us for our now reduced ration of food. The British were battle-weary and less well fed than their American colleagues. Their surly behaviour struck a sour note. Across from the front gate of our former prison the British set up a death camp where they placed wounded horses from the Japanese cavalry and provided no food or water. Here I heard an injured horse give a soft groan as he slowly lowered his head to crop a single blade of grass from the hard mud of the compound. I wondered how people from the green land of Jeremy Fisher could bear to force a wounded horse to starve and die of thirst, even in a foreign place. As I looked through the woven bamboo fence a Japanese soldier came and brushed some flies from an open sore on the horse's shoulder. His eyes met mine in a look of fatalistic understanding. Here we were, both powerless to stop this fresh atrocity, both at the end of our time in China.

27. Last Days in Shanghai

While my mother was waiting to have the operation to remove her gall bladder, we moved to be near the hospital. We also caught up on my father's news about what happened after the Chinese welcomed him and his fellow prisoners to Peking.

At about 2:00 a.m. the convoy of trucks taking the prisoners from Fengtai, which is where the Haiphong Road people had been held after they left Shanghai, arrived at a Peking hotel. The dazed and starving men went to actual beds. The dream continued the next day as the Japanese hustled them into baths and showers – *baths and showers* – so that they would be presentable when the United Nations Mission arrived on August 22.

Then the Japanese carried in some American airmen. Beaten and starved, they had dysentery. The Japanese had not allowed the men to go to a lavatory, take off their clothes or wash. Instead, the Japanese hosed them down from time to time and the airmen's leather clothes had shrunk tightly around their bodies, adding to the torture. Listening to my father, I wondered how the Japanese soldiers could be so different from the people we saw on holidays to Japan; and thought that maybe the type of brutal treatment we had seen, of Japanese soldiers convalescing from war wounds, made them treat their enemy counterparts with such depraved cruelty.

On the following days, Chinese people appeared with gifts of cooked food and cakes.

On August 22, the United Nations Mission team of six men led by an American, Major Nichols, arrived in Peking. They gave white bread, fruit and honey to the former prisoners. And wonder of wonders, "… *special American parcels dropped from the air.*" On August 23, the Mission went to Fengtai and reported on the conditions there.

My father told us that in Peking he had enjoyed the same kind attention and medical care from the Americans as we were receiving in Shanghai. He and the others had the privilege of entering the Forbidden City where China's emperors lived. There they saw a trove of wonderful artistic treasure in the form of carvings and paintings. Some had been literally the life's work of the artists, who had carved and painted intricate scenes, with individual faces on each person. The prisoners then went to an American hospital ship, the USS Lavaca, for over a month to recuperate, as their rescuers thought it would be too much of a shock for families to see their husbands and fathers in the state they were in.

On the day our mother went into hospital our father went with her and they said Gordon and I could go to a film show downtown. This was the first time we had gone out alone into Shanghai and it was a big adventure. We settled ourselves down in the Cathay on Avenue Joffre in the French Concession. To start there was a lengthy newsreel, which was really a documentary, giving a retrospect of the war in Europe and the Far East.

For the first time I found out about the concentration camps in Germany. On the screen appeared an image of two children electrocuted on a fence, lying stiff and white like carved wooden figures. One still held a doll in her arms. Walking skeletons with skin stretched over their bones and ghastly smiles on their faces came out of a Japanese forced labour mining camp. A Chinese girl bound to a chair lay dead after being raped by dozens of Japanese soldiers. A press photo of Nanking showed narrow streets choked with bodies, faces down, hands clawed forward, feet stretched out ready to run even in death.

In Japan, women practised throwing bamboo spears. Children practised, carrying explosives in their satchels and darting out of hiding so that they too could become suicide bombers if Japan were to be invaded. Across China black smoke belched from chimneys of hospitals where Chinese civilians had been subjected to vivisection, without anaesthetics, and their bodies burned. Japanese planes rained down bombs, and also infectious diseases, on Chinese towns and villages. Rivers overflowed with the dead. The Japanese had slaughtered many millions of Chinese. One authority, Chalmers Johnson, estimates 30 million were murdered in the Co-Prosperity Sphere, of whom 23 million people were ethnic Chinese.

I couldn't pay attention to the movie that followed for thinking of the ghastly scenes and information in the newsreel. That night I dreamed of Japanese surgeons discussing how many "logs" (Chinese) they had "cut" (murdered) that day. In the dream two bright red streams of blood shot up from the neck of a civilian beheaded at random in the street. I woke up screaming.

After that our parents decided that we must go on visits to the city only with an adult. Gordon and I and our father divided our time between visiting my mother and sightseeing across Shanghai. While showing us round, our father emphasized Shanghai's role of leadership within China.

First we visited some places on the Bund. No.3 the Bund was the Shanghai Club, haunt of the big business *taipans* and there we saw the longest bar in the world at thirty feet long. Then we went to see the famous Customs House clock, called locally Big Ching, a replica of London's Big Ben. Our father told us it had struck every quarter of an hour since 1893. He also mentioned that the playwright Noel Coward had written his play *Private Lives* at the Cathay Hotel just north of the Bund on Nanking Road.

Before we left we made one last sentimental trip to the Race Course. I felt sad as the grounds had been neglected. Everywhere we looked, there were tangled grass and waist-high weeds, with discarded Japanese army tin plates and bottles lying in the undergrowth. The racecourse and tennis courts, cricket fields, baseball diamonds and lawn bowling greens were all overgrown. It was hard to see where anything had been. I did recognize a building my mother had shown me before the attack. Then (it seemed like eons ago), attached high up on a wall, were a cutout wooden moon and stars. They were to be lit up that night, and my parents were going to a dinner and dance on the lawn.

The stands stood out, with holes in the roof and broken seating. I rebelled against the decay, narrowed my eyes and willed myself to *see* the Shanghai Municipal Police sports day, which had been held at the racecourse each summer.

There suddenly in the seating were the crowds of wives and children of the police force, dressed in their summer clothes, chattering excitedly and waving programs. Under an endless high blue sky everyone was watching the parade of the turbaned Sikhs, mounted on the distinctive Mongolian ponies, which were always used for horse racing in Shanghai. The Sikhs carried their lances tipped by colourful silk pennants fluttering in the breeze from their passing. The police had turned out in force, thousands of men of several races, white, oriental and East Indian, in their summer whites. Tea, small cakes, and sandwiches, fruit and ices were being served in the clubhouse. White clad Chinese servants moved discreetly about, catering to every need.

The competitions themselves took place on the racetrack, in an atmosphere of tremendous good humour. I ran again in the race for children. The older ones were handicapped: they began the race at the starting line. Younger children stood at various distances nearer the finish, according to size. We all started to run the race together and dashed to the finishing line where everyone was given a prize of a small bag of sweets. The organizers also pinned a medal, with a red ribbon, on each child who had run the race. I then rushed off to find my father, sometimes dismayed at clinging to the wrong white trouser leg, before finding him at last. ...

I came back to the present with a jolt, as I realised that now, I would be winding my arms about our father above his waist. It seemed appropriate that my last memory of Shanghai should be of this, the quintessential public event of the dying foreign presence.

One cold morning in February 1946, we hugged Ah Ling and Ah Fok. For the last time, placing her hands round either side of my head (a wonderful feeling) Ah Ling whispered, "Margaret go sleep well tonight." I wondered when I would ever see her again.

Then we went to board our ship for Britain. It was originally a Royal Mail Line passenger/freight ship converted for the transport of troops, the HMS Highland Chieftain, and would take us on a hazardous journey through mined seas. I carried the mandatory lifejacket on which my father had drawn a little pig (in a lifejacket) bravely about to jump off the railing of a boat. As we drove to the docks I looked up at the Race Course building where the cutout wooden moon had hung and long since been dismantled. I half expected to see there a cutout version of ourselves – to be destroyed after we'd gone.

In the taxi, my parents were already reminiscing about times with their brothers and sisters, and were obviously looking forward to the return to their native land. My brother still had vague memories of aunts and uncles he'd met on a trip back to Britain before I was born. But I was *leaving* the land of my birth, and losing again my beloved Chinese mother, Ah Ling. I couldn't explain the feeling of bereavement. But in my heart I felt I was going into exile.

We passed the usual throng of shoppers, pickpockets and prostitutes, rickshaw coolies and beggars. Sidewalk stalls were selling black market medical- and food-aid, sent by the United States for the Chinese people. A new element, the young American servicemen, gamboled in their midst, throwing around their "gold" dollars, the only solid currency in Shanghai. As if to make up for lost time, the lighted signs along Nanking Road and the Bund were now on all day. The neon outline of Sincere's department store glittered its message of triumphant commercialism. Shanghai's ultra modern, cosmopolitan life had resumed.

All the old wheeler-dealers were out in force, well able to bear and profit from the stress and competition of the city. They were putting to good use the foreigners' cars and other property they had commandeered. Already they had levelled the British cemetery on Bubbling Well Road and were building over it. Our Anglican, Holy Trinity Cathedral was now a factory manufacturing ballpoint pens.

As we went up the gangway of HMS Highland Chieftain, in one hand I carried Mrs. Duncan's bag with my books in it. The bag's bright colours were faded now, and just after the war's end Mrs. Duncan had died. Over my shoulder hung the worn but still friendly head of the blue giraffe; he was continuing as loyal companion on the next journey of my life. As we boarded, the city's *jenao*, hot din, was in full swing; it had barely missed a beat.

Under a darkening sky the ship pulled away; the low grey clouds rolled out beyond the reach of our eyes all the way that we were going: along the Whangpoo, across the Yangtze, to the roiling brown waves of the China Sea. And engrossed in its own affairs Shanghai, the love of my life, the place of my birth, turned its back.

On the wharf, a dead seagull, its wing lifted by fitful gusts of wind, waved goodbye.

Author's Note

Like all great cities Shanghai had its dark side. It came to be called the Paris of the East, the Whore of Asia. However, Aldous Huxley writing in the 1930s called Shanghai, "Life itself. Nothing more intensely living can be imagined." It is ironic that the soul and flesh of such a remarkable place should vanish so quickly after the Communist take-over of 1949.

Only the bones are left: the magnificent buildings, the head offices and consulates, the hotels and clubs of Shanghai's Bund, and of its central city. These are now taken up by different people and different uses, the polish faded under dust and grime, the immaculate lawns obliterated under hastily-built housing, the foreign residents thrown out, the capitalists, gangsters, gamblers and professionals executed. Although another type of modernity is returning in Pootung, and new entertainments are offered in some of the old buildings, old Shanghai: the Paris of the East, the Whore of Asia, Life itself, no longer exists.

I have never returned to Shanghai. I feel I never can, not to the Shanghai I knew. A televised memoir of Dame Margot Fonteyn, the distinguished former pupil of the Cathedral

Girls' School, showed its building now being used as a theatre school. The stairs and wood-paneled walls looked unpolished and neglected. The structure is one of the relics of the pre-Communist city that have been absorbed and put to use. Reports from friends who have been there recently only confirm the rightness of my decision. Neither the drab Shanghai of the early Chinese Communists, nor the new modernity of the buildings in Pootung, bears much relation to the glittering cosmopolitan city of the 1930s. However, through my reminiscences and reading, I have been able to visit Shanghai as it was then; and that must satisfy me.

Epilogue

For the expatriate civilians interned there, the International Settlement really did prove to be a *gudao* (lone islet) of safety, in that their death rate during imprisonment was lower than that of Allied civilians interned by the Japanese in other places. This was no doubt because some diplomats, such as the Swiss and Dutch – but not the British – stayed in Shanghai during the Japanese occupation. The Japanese did not want to lose face by having others see their atrocities.

The Individuals

In August of 1941 Major Bourne, the former commissioner of the SMC police, left Shanghai with his family. He spent the rest of the war in North America, away from the active war zones, at a desk position.

In 1942, the British Ambassador, Sir Archibald Clark Kerr, left Shanghai on a Japanese ship evacuating diplomats and others. Like Bourne, he spent the rest of the war behind the battle lines, in a diplomatic posting to Russia. Both Commissioner Bourne and Ambassador Clark Kerr were instrumental in urging others, especially the Shanghai Municipal Police, to stay in the path of the Japanese army, which was known to be incredibly brutal. British authorities did not honour promises to evacuate families. The object was to keep order, obtain a smooth transition to Japanese rule and thus protect valuable British commercial interests from being destroyed or looted in potential rioting.

Arnold Kiehn, the American who had given a home to our dog Dopey, was repatriated along with others in a 1943 exchange of prisoners, but returned to Shanghai after the war.

The Chinese Nationalist government, anxious to be rid of foreigners, would not allow overseas banks to function in China. But Arnold was interested in buying my father's clandestinely made sketches of life in Haiphong Road prison and Fengtai; in Hong Kong he also sold for us some family items of value. So through Arnold, my father obtained American currency to reward our special people, Ah Fok and Ah Ling, for their loyalty, bravery and kindness to us. With her money, Ah Ling immediately bought several gold rings.

We never saw our Chinese servants again. As our parents were concerned about the advance of the Communists in China we did not write. Militarily, the Communists had succeeded in the countryside round Shanghai. The Nationalists' disastrous handling of the economy was the last straw. It seemed clear the Communists would prevail and that it would become dangerous for our former servants to be in contact with Westerners.

Arnold Kiehn stayed in China for a while, and we saw a newspaper item in the 1950s saying he had escaped from a Communist prison, suffering from beri beri. The Lewises also stayed in China for a few years, although Mrs. Lewis divided her time between Britain and Shanghai. Their daughter, Kathleen, returned to Britain: to boarding school in Scotland. In 1951 Neilson had the bad luck to knock down a Chinese man who had run out in front of his car "beating the devil" but had not managed to get out of the way in time. The Chinese man suffered a broken leg and Neilson spent two months in a crowded Chinese prison until the Chinese man's leg healed. When this ordeal ended he returned to Scotland.

After the war Doreen Hunt and, I believe, Betty Kyte went to the United States. The Hunt and Sanbrook fathers became skilled carpenters, much in demand in the local construction industry in California. Jack Sanbrook inculcated a strong work ethic in his children. At the age of 28, John became the youngest County Counsel in California. His younger siblings, George and later born sister Irene, also became lawyers and practiced together. Like my father and many other ex-internees of the Japanese of their age, the Hunt and Sanbrook fathers died suddenly in their early fifties. Abe Abraham lives in Los Angeles.

My last news of Doreen Hunt was that she was getting married after completing high school, and of Isabel Gomersall that she had attended boarding school in England and later married a Bostonian, going to live in the United States. To my knowledge, all the other internees mentioned in this memoir returned to Britain. Tony Corner became a distinguished mathematician in the field of Algebra, with a chair at Oxford. Kathleen Lewis attended St Andrews University, married John Lisle, a nuclear physicist and academic, becoming Kay Lisle, and lives with her family in Cheshire. The Grants returned to Hastings and now live with their families in various parts of England. Aunt Haruko and Uncle Steve Wilkinson went to Eritrea for a while before returning to the south of England to retire. Aunt Haruko lived at Bexhill in England, and died there at the age of 93 in August of 2002. Jose Chamberlain stayed in Mrs. Toon's flat until her father returned in October. Jose's father spent some years in Germany with the Control Commission, going to England to spend as much time as he could with Jose who was in boarding school there. Jose became a senior manager with Pfizer. She died in 2014 after a long battle with cancer, during which she kept in touch with many fellow internees whom she regarded as a surrogate family.

The Jesuits of Zikawei continued their activities until 1950 when their whole complex was taken over by the Chinese Communists. They left a legacy. The observatory became the Shanghai Municipal Meteorological Department and one of their language buildings became the Shanghai Institute of Foreign Languages.

After the war, Zhang Shankun relocated to Hong Kong where unlike many other Chinese filmmakers he refused to sell out to the mainland Communists. Instead, in 1949, he re-established his company under the original Xinhua (New China Movie Company) name. Until his death in 1956 aged 51, Zhang concentrated on improving colour photography in films, and also shooting them in foreign locations, namely Japan and Taiwan.

Also after the war a Chinese court sentenced Lawrence Kentwell to seven years in prison.

Like the others, my brother and I went to the grey post-war British world of rationing and shortages, to the inconceivable, damp cold of the climate. We also encountered the bitter, Calvinistic character of the Scots. After the technicolour tones of Shanghai, I now began to live my life in black-and-white.

"The air is grey, here," I said to my mother. "Even the air is grey." For many years the feeling of nostalgia lingered. It has never really gone away.

Our health was not good just after the war and, because of this, my father relocated us from Glasgow, where we had relatives, to a small town outside. During the record-breaking, stone-hard winter of 1946/47, the deep pond of my teacher, Miss Young, froze solid and all her carp died.

After some months, possibly a year, spent recovering from his ordeal, our father went to North Africa, with the British Army rank of major, to help organize the flow of refugees. During this time, he paid to the British government what they had charged for our food after the war's end and for our transport back to Britain. After over a year our father returned to a position in the British civil service and helped set up the National Health Service in Scotland.

I had the impression that there were financial difficulties, in particular at the start, and also after my father died. However, our parents never discussed these problems with me, nor did they discuss the war, Japan's reign of terror in China, or their opinion of the actions of the individuals and governments involved. They may have thought my brother and I were too young; they may also have felt we had enough to do in adjusting to a new country without being harassed by thoughts of our family's past experiences.

Later in life, our mother became president for

Scotland of the Women Citizens, and through this body had the antiquated law in Scotland with respect to women substantially changed.

Like our father, my brother attended Glasgow School of Art and has retired from a career as a designer of carpets for hotels and historical buildings. Also, he is a talented actor and singer, playing the lead for the Glasgow Light Opera for many years. Gordon has received awards for his playbill designs and an award, for 50 years of dedicated service to Amateur Theatre, from Britain's National Operatic and Dramatic Society. He is married with four children and nine grandchildren. I attended Glasgow University completing an MA in History. There I met my husband who has now retired from the University of Toronto faculty. I have had three careers: in high school teaching, (social and financial) marketing research after completing an MBA at the University of Toronto, and also as the mother of three children who have three children of their own.

Our camp's last commandant, Mr. Hashimoto, and guards returned to Japan. Aunt Haruko, who had relatives in Japan, told me that our commandant committed suicide by having his best friend behead him. Thanks to the perseverance of some internees, one of whom was Betty Kyte's father, two guards implicated in the murder of William Hutton were tried and found guilty. The doctors, who carried out the vivisection of hundreds of thousands of Chinese civilians without anaesthesia, also returned to Japan and lived out their lives with high honour and achieving senior positions. They gave the Americans their research notes, and paid no penalty for their crimes.

Prince Asaka, who supervised the Rape of Nanking,

lived through his life with no penalty for his actions during the war.

Our father died in 1953 at the age of 54, and our mother in 1964, aged 65. There was a high early death rate among the former prisoners: Looking at British and Commonwealth males taken prisoner in China after 1941, of those 35-45 at the time of their imprisonment, 70 percent had died by 1955. i.e. did not reach the age of 60. However, there are many grandchildren, and great-grandchildren, all blessedly free of yearnings for other times and places or worries about war.

The Nations

For salaries and pensions due to them, the British government referred the Shanghai Municipal Police officers to the Anglo-Chinese Treaty of 11th January 1943. This treaty was between the British government and the Nationalist Chinese. In it the British gave away to the Nationalists all the assets and liabilities of the Shanghai Municipal Council. Chiang Kai-shek did not honour these responsibilities.

The British government representatives also pointed out that, unlike Hong Kong, to whose police internees the British government had given salaries and pensions owed them, the International Settlement was not a colony (and in particular after the January 1943 treaty, was not part of British responsibilities) and SMC people did not deserve such remuneration. This was the same government whose representative, Ambassador Sir Archibald Clark Kerr, had told my father in 1939 (and and no doubt others) that it would be disloyal, even treasonable (a hanging offence) to the Empire, if they resigned their SMC posts to offer their services on British territory within the Commonwealth. Although there is strong written proof to the contrary, these British authorities denied having exhorted their citizens to stay in the path of the Japanese as their duty to the Empire.

Before 1945 courage, honour and loyalty in service to the British Empire, even at the expense of personal survival, still held a place. For some, this sacrifice was for others, not themselves. Afterwards, these ideas, and the Empire itself, crumbled.

The Russians took over Manchuria and handed it, along with highly trained captured Japanese troops and their modern armaments, to the Chinese Communists. The Japanese then trained and armed the Communist troops. The way the situation in China developed was another tragedy for the Chinese people. They escaped the clutches of Japan only to be handed over to another mass murderer: Mao.

The Americans and Japanese kept secret a huge war booty looted by the Japanese across the Co-Prosperity Sphere. After peace, America claimed the Japanese Emperor was an innocent prisoner of military interests, and said they were concerned that the payment of reparations would harm the Japanese economy, and turn Japan, that they portrayed as a poor country, towards Communism. Despite the remarkable resurgence of the Japanese economy, the United States designed the 1951 San Francisco Treaty of Peace with Japan to eliminate any possibility of war reparations. However, the Dutch refused to sign without the addition of a disclaimer, called the Seeker Accord, to allow individuals to seek redress from Japan. In 2001 the Japanese High Court unilaterally rejected this accord.

British negotiators at the Treaty of San Francisco had Article 26 inserted into the treaty. Article 26 allows those states signing the 1951 treaty to claim similar benefits for their citizens as those granted in subsequent peace treaties. The later Burmese/Japanese and Swiss/Japanese treaties activated Article 26. However, British Foreign Office bureaucrats decided not to seek similar benefits for British subjects and recorded this decision in a memo now filed in the UK National Archives in FO 371/115281. ... *We should not of course give any publicity to this decision. Legal advisers agree.* The then Minister, Lord Reading endorsed the memo, adding that pressure on Japan ... *would be likely to cause the maximum of resentment for the minimum of advantage.*

In the late 1990s ABCIFER (Association of British Civilian Internees Far East Region) discovered the Foreign Office internal memos and prepared to take action of their own in international courts, legal opinion being that there was no time limit on Article 26. However, Prime Minister Blair, concerned about bad publicity for the government, before a visit by the Japanese Emperor and an impending election, made what was in effect an out of court settlement. He assigned £10,000 in compensation to each of those (few) former prisoners of the Japanese still alive at that time, although some were denied this because they were deemed to be not British enough. (For a time, ABCIFER'S struggle continued on their behalf - unsuccessfully.)

This compensation was made to look like a gift, rather than the as-of-right debt of honour that it was. The British government announced it as being given on the grounds of the extremely high death rate among Allied prisoners: on the average over 25 percent in the Japanese camps in three and one-half years, versus three to four percent in German camps in six years. Of course within that average, the death rate for Allied Prisoners of War (members of armed forces) held by Japan was very high, at almost 40 percent. The corresponding death rate for those held by Germany was one percent. The British authorities still refused any responsibility for having insisted that their citizens should stay in the path of danger. After the election, they even went back on their blanket promise of compensation, and withdrew it for those ex-internees who had not lived in Britain for at least 20 years.

The United States has consistently opposed forcing Japan to pay reparations to anyone, even to their own slave labourers of the Japanese and "comfort women," (young women of the occupied territories, in the main kidnapped, and used as prostitutes by the Japanese soldiers); it keeps many of its post-war files related to Japan classified.

All observers agree that the Japanese murdered a huge number of people in the Co-Prosperity Sphere. Their main target was ethnic Chinese. Professor Chalmers Johnson estimated the Japanese murdered 23 million ethnic Chinese within the Co-Prosperity Sphere. Unlike Germany, Japan did not apologize or pay reparations, due in particular to the Chinese and other Far Eastern people they had persecuted. Instead, the Japanese leaders quickly devised a face-saving propaganda campaign using Hiroshima and Nagasaki, portraying themselves both at home and abroad as victims, and rewriting the history of what went before. Japan actually denied, at first, any massacres of Chinese in Nanking where they murdered by hand over twice as many people as died in the atomic bombings of Hiroshima and Nagasaki.

The Chinese Communist government did not strongly pursue the matters of reparations, and an apology and admission of guilt from Japan. This would have detracted from their policy of demonizing Europeans and Americans. Also Mao Tse Tung expressed a perverted kind of gratitude to Japan whom he regarded as having defeated the Nationalists. The compliance of the Allies and their refusal to release information has enabled the Japanese propaganda machine of denial both within and outside Japan.

To avoid criticism the Japanese continue to hide behind Hiroshima and Nagasaki, and even to deny their own violent acts. The 2002 legal hearings in Tokyo confirmed atrocities at Unit 731 in Manchuria, where Chinese advocates showed that Japanese doctors conducted the vivisection of over 250,000 unanaesthetized Chinese prisoners. In August a Tokyo district court dismissed the case and said it had no legal basis. Victims' families will receive no apology and no compensation.

Currently (2008) the Japanese authorities are denying the evidence from books such as Iris Chang's *The Rape of Nanking*, which is not circulated in Japan, and in 2005 brought out school textbooks virtually erasing what little content they had previously included on this period, as it does not lead to pride in one's country. This caused riots in major cities of China and South Korea. Recently, the Japanese Prime Minister Abe stated, untruly, that all the "comfort women" were professional prostitutes. The Japanese are also asking for an expansion of their armed forces. Understandably, other nations (notably China and Korea) do not trust the idea of a more powerful Japan.

This collective denial of the past, among the political

leaders of Japan and the former Allied countries, will continue to have consequences for us all.

NOTE

Recently, risking their own safety, a group of older Japanese citizens, some of them former soldiers, has set up the privately funded Chukiren Peace Memorial Museum. Located in a remote part of Japan, this is a resource for scholars and to educate local children in what happened in the Second World War.

Kubota Hisao (86) former soldier, "Japanese people talk about the sufferings of atomic bomb attacks and air raids, but we need to understand them in the context of Japan's war of aggression."

To read David McNeill's article about the museum, Google David McNeill, the African-Pacific Journal, "A Footsoldier in the War Against Forgetting Japanese Wartime Atrocities.

Acknowledgements in alphabetical order

For their excellent editorial advice my sincere thanks go to Meg Masters and Meg Taylor. Jackie Kaiser recommended them.

I also owe much to the tough critiques and support of the University Women's Club of Toronto's writing group ably led by Marianne Brandis, who always advises sensibly: Marilyn Ashby, Dorothy Bremner, Karin Brothers, Catherine Cooper, Liz de Corneille, Charmay Crane, Edra Ferguson, Lynn Friesen, Sandra Gentles, Irene Hinchcliffe, Margaret Macdonald and Sadie Stren.

In chronological order as they helped with this memoir, first I thank our children, Katherine, Isabel and Gordon, whose questions prompted me to write the account at last. Thanks go to Isabel in particular for her encouragement and also guidance, and my niece Elizabeth Young and friends Margaret Aanders, Ann Abouchar, Sandra Badov, Beth Bentley, Susan Kent Davidson, Lesley Duncan, Alan Grant, Isabel Highet, Carol Mark, Ann Moon, Connie Sword, Inga Tarshis, Helen Thompson, Dorothy and Bill Trimble, for their encouragement. I thank also Donald Grant, my brother Gordon Telfer, and Aunt Haruko Wilkinson for their input to the content and their encouragement.

I salute Dr. Greg Leck, the ultimate authority (to whom I was introduced by Ron Davie) and cannot thank him enough for providing correct information about the camps in Shanghai, and Kay Lisle who knows where everything is in Shanghai and remembers when events took place. Ron Bridge, president of ABCIFER has helped publicize this book to other survivors, and has provided crucial information; Jose Chamberlain, who was in the same camps as myself, read and corrected the text. Any errors are my own.

Very special thanks go to my husband for his help in finding information sources and for his tolerance and understanding of the time I have spent in writing this story.

Finally, I thank those who were so kind as to take the time to read and comment on the book: Ron Bridge, Modris Eksteins, Greg Leck and Betty Jane Wylie.

Q & A with Margaret Blair

Q 1.

You started with a narrow account, for your family, of your experiences in 1930s and 1940s Shanghai. However, you substantially broadened the scope to create the book you have now. What motivated you?

There were several motivations. First, I felt the usual account omitted information on what was going on outside the writer's city or internment camp. Also, as I read more, I was concerned about how little I had known before. For instance, previously I had a vague impression that the International Settlement was a colony: I'd never even heard of the Land Regulations for Treaty Ports. I came to the conclusion that my memoir should have a larger scope than the usual story of internment by the Japanese.

Secondly, I was horrified at the Chinese Holocaust and concerned that I knew virtually nothing about it until taking up my own writing task. The media concentrated on Hiroshima and Nagasaki. There was little or no information about the other side of the story of the Pacific World War II: what horrors the Chinese had suffered. Also, I found there was a third area of conflict: that between the Communists and Nationalists in China. Throughout the memoir, and in a concise way, I've tried to bring out the several sides of the story of what happened during the war.

Third, accounts of the cosmopolitan, modern, pre-war city of Shanghai fascinated me. I had lived there, but previously knew so little about it, and believed accounts of Treaty Port life, for both foreigners and Chinese, should be included in my memoir as they would be of interest to others.

Fourthly, there are few people now alive who remember these events and places. Much has been written up in academic books (both Western and Japanese) which few read as they are not very accessible, partly because they are in academic libraries and partly because they are written in a style that is not readily understood by the ordinary reading public. I would like to make this information more available to the public in general.

Q 2.
Why do you think you were so ill-informed about Pacific World War II?

For good and kind reasons, my parents didn't discuss, and distracted us from, the wartime experiences.

There was another factor, affecting information for everyone, and that was the cover-up of what the Japanese did. As soon as (in the 1930s) the Japanese noticed international disapproval of their actions in the Far East, their governments started a strong and so far (2008) unrelenting propaganda campaign of denial. This was backed by the Allies (in particular the United States) who feared Japan would join the USSR.

However, there is a third factor, and that is (particularly in N. America) the media's not meeting their responsibilities in investigating and reporting on the Chinese Holocaust. I mentioned the inaccessibility of academic studies to the public, but it is not academics that are expected to inform the general public, it is the media. The media are the people who communicate most directly with the general public.

Q 3.
In your Epilogue you deal in more depth, than is usual for a memoir such as yours, with the aftermath of the war to the present day. Wouldn't it have been preferable, and neater, to end with the dead seagull waving goodbye, and with your Afterword?

I think not (not preferable, not neater). As a child I was impressed with how the tragedies of World War I continued to affect and be remembered by those who survived, in particular for the Scottish branch of my family.

In the 1930s World War I was very much a presence generally. Wars don't just stop and then everyone returns to normal. They continue to have an effect. For World War II, I believe this is more true of the Pacific war than of the European. In the Pacific apologies and amends were not made and there was actually a concerted effort by the powers involved, on both sides, to cover up. If you want to see Holocaust denial, study what happened to the Chinese from 1931 to the present. One example is the petty attacks from Western academics, and threats by the Japanese right wing, against Iris Chang author of *The Rape of Nanking*.

Q 4. In writing *Gudao, Lone Islet*, have you satisfied your own curiosity and interest in the further writing about China?

Indeed No: One area on which I touch in *Gudao* is the wonderful burgeoning of a modern literary and visual media culture centred largely in Shanghai. In my next book, *Shanghai Scarlet*, I shall explore this further through the lives of real people. The Japanese occupation and warfare between rival political and criminal factions in China had a tragic effect on their lives. This will be a tale of love, intrigue and murder.

Q 5. Tell me more about your next book.
My new book, *Shanghai Scarlet,* provides a riveting recreation of Old Shanghai in all its exhilaration, degradation and danger, as a talented modernist writer and sophisticated courtesan meet, intertwine their lives and attempt to keep their love alive during a time of political turmoil.

Shanghai Scarlet is a compelling story with excellent pacing and an extraordinary, haunting, even terrifying, conclusion.

Readers' Comments on *Shanghai Scarlet*

"Margaret Blair's depth of character development is indeed impressive. . . . she has brought these characters to life for the reader, (and) ... has really captured the spirit of Shanghai of that time. *Shanghai Scarlet* is a fascinating story, which makes for compelling reading, ... a wonderful evocation of a bygone era, one sure to appeal to many readers."

John Meehan SJ, professor of history, Campion College, University of Regina, author, *Chasing the Dragon in Shanghai*

I greatly appreciate your focus on Qiu Peipei who, as you say, has not been studied much, but the significance of her life, and romance with Mu, shed important light on the times.

This is a sensitive, thoughtful and poignant story. The ending is very effective. It is hard not to be touched by the heroine's love for her husband and to worry about her fate ...

Poshek Fu, professor of history, University of Illinois, Urbana-Champaign, author of *Passivity, Resistance and Collaboration, Intellectual Choices in Occupied Shanghai, 1937-1949*

"... a dazzling novel based on pre-revolutionary Shanghai, where Margaret Blair was born."

Bettyjane Wylie C.M. award winning author

Suggested Discussion for Book Clubs

At public addresses I have given and in messages from readers, people have mentioned that *Gudao, Lone Islet,* would be a wonderful book for book clubs. I realized the book had many points for discussion and that it raises topics for further study. In the West there is a burgeoning interest in the Far East in general and in Shanghai in particular. Therefore I've prepared some book club discussion questions.

If anyone from a book club would like to add to these questions, please feel free to e-mail me at my website: www. margaretblair.com

1. In what way did the lives of Chinese and foreigners in the international concessions impinge upon each other?

2. What effect did the many foreign areas and culture have on the development of Chinese political and literary culture?

3. How did the Chinese cultural renaissance in Shanghai's Treaty Port vary from that in colonial territories such as India?

4. Compare and contrast the characters of Margaret and Gordon. In what way did their different personalities affect the way in which they reacted to the changes in their lives after December 1941 to the end of the war?

5. What, in your opinion, were the different motivations of individuals and groups who collaborated with the Japanese?

6. The memoir starts just before the Japanese occupation, and yet the reader receives solid information about previous events. What techniques does the author use to achieve this?

7. *Gudao, Lone Islet* is written from the point of view of a very young girl and yet again the text includes much that only an adult would know about. How has the author inserted the adult material?

8. What effect does the seagull waving goodbye have on the reader and what is its meaning?

Areas for Further Study

- The multi-faceted life in cosmopolitan Old Shanghai and its underworld
- The rise up to 1937 of a modern literary and movie culture in China based primarily in Shanghai
- The course of World War II in the Pacific
- The implications of the San Francisco Treaty of 1951 – for the Far Eastern countries and the rest of the world.

Bibliography

Peggy Abkhazi, *A Curious Cage: A Shanghai Journal 1941-45*, Edited and with an introduction by S.W.Jackman, Sono Nis Press 1981, Victoria, British Columbia Canada.

Barbara Baker, *Shanghai, Electric and Lurid City,* Oxford University Press, 1998

Herbert Bix, *Hirohito and the Making of Modern Japan,* Perennial (Harper-Collins) 2001, New York

Major K.M.Bourne, Letter (undated) in the British Public Record Office, London

Timothy Brook, "Collaborationist Nationalism in Occupied Wartime China", *Nation Work,* ed Timothy Brook and Andre Schmid, The University of Michigan Press, Ann Arbor 2000

Timothy Brook, *Collaboration,* Harvard University Press, 2005

Dora Sanders Carney, *Foreign Devils Had Light Eyes, A Memoir of Shanghai 1933-1939*, Dorset Publishing Inc. 1980, Toronto: Virgo Press (a division of Panama Press Ltd.) 1981

Iris Chang, *The Rape of Nanking*, Basic Books, A Subsidiary of Perseus Books, L.L.C. New York 1997

Steven C. Clemons, The New York Times, September 4, 2001, "Recovering Japan's Wartime Past – and Ours"

Warren Cohen, Times Literary Supplement, August 19 & 26 2005, "Bitter surrender", a review of *Racing the Enemy* by Tsuyoshi Hasegawa, Harvard University Press 2005

Modris Eksteins, *Walking Since Daybreak A Story of Eastern Europe, World War II and the Heart of Our Century*, Key Porter Books, Toronto 1999

Jack Edwards, in collaboration with Jimmy Walker *Banzai, You Bastards!*, Souvenir Press, London 1991

John King Fairbank, *The Great Chinese Revolution 1800-95*, Harper and Row, New York 1986

Niall Ferguson, *Empire – How Britain Made the Modern World*, Allen Lane, The Penguin Press, London 2003

Martin Gilbert, *Second World War* Phoenix, Division of Orion Books Ltd. London 1995

Katherine Gordon, *A Curious Life – The Biography of Princess Peggy Abkhazi*, Sono Nis Press, Winlaw, B.C. 2002

Gow's Guide to Shanghai (1924)

Graham Hutchings, Times Literary Supplement, July 10 1998 "Strangers on the Shore", a review of *No Dogs and Not many Chinese - Treaty Port life in China*, 1843-1943 by Frances Wood pub. John Murray, London.

Chalmers Johnson, London Review of Books, November 2003 "The Looting of Asia", a review of *Gold Warriors: America's Secret Recovery of Yamashita's Gold* by Sterling Seagrave and Peggy Seagrave, Verso 2003

Paul Kennedy, *The Rise and Fall of the Great Powers*, Random House, New York 1987

Greg Leck, *Captives of Empire: The Japanese Internment of Allied Civilians in China, 1941-1945*, Shandy Press, 2006

Leo Ou-fan Lee, *Shanghai Modern. The Flowering of a New Urban Culture in Shanghai* 1930-1945, Harvard University Press, Cambridge Massachusetts 1999

Urban C. Lehner, Wall Street Journal, September 8 1998, *"Changed History – More Japanese Deny Nation was Aggressor During World War II"*

Pan Ling, *In Search of Old Shanghai*, Hong Kong Joint Publishing Co. Inc. 1982

Penelope Lively, *Oleander Jacaranda. A Childhood Perceived, A Memoir*, Harper Collins, New York 1994

Hanchao Lu, *Beyond the Neon Lights, Everyday Shanghai in the Early Twentieth Century,* University of California Press, 1999

David McNeill, *A Foot Soldier in the War Against Forgetting Japanese Wartime Atrocities www. japanfocus.org/products/ details/2333*

Anthony and Peter Miall, *The Victorian Nursery Book,* J.M.Dent & Sons, Ltd., London 1980

Harriet Sergeant, *Shanghai,* Jonathon Cape Ltd., London 1991

Standard Guide Book, *All About Shanghai and Environs,* The University Press, Shanghai Edition 1934-35

Jonathan Spence New York Review of Books, May 28 1998 "Goodfellas in Shanghai", a review by Jonathan Spence of *The Shanghai Badlands*: *Wartime Terrorism and Urban Crisis, 1937–41* by Frederic Wakeman Jr. pub. Cambridge University Press.

James Trager ed. *The People's Chronology,* Henry Holt and Company, New York 1992

Frederic Wakeman Jr., *The Shanghai Badlands*: *Wartime Terrorism and Urban Crisis 1937–41,* Cambridge University Press, 1998

Wen-hsin Yeh (editor) *Wartime Shanghai,* Routledge, London 1998

February 2, 1997 newsletter of The Center For Internee Rights, Inc. 6060 La Gorce Drive, Miami Beach, Florida 33140-2117

Tel: (305) 864-2558 Fax: (305) 861-8550

The Globe and Mail, January 2, 1999, *Japan Pariah of the Pacific*, Nicholas Kristof

National Post, December 7th, 2000 "Details of horrifying experiments put Japan at war with its history (Trial unearths how thousands were tortured)" Peter Goodspeed

Printed in the United States
By Bookmasters